UNF*CKING PRIVATE HEALTHCARE

The Playbook on Owning Your Dream Practice

Daniel Tribby

Unf*cking Private Healthcare: The Playbook on Owning Your Dream Practice
Copyright © 2020 Daniel Tribby

ISBN: 979-8-68096-292-3

No part of this publication may be reproduced, stored in a retrieval system or transmitted in any form or any means electronic, mechanical, photocopying, scanning, recording, or otherwise.

All rights reserved including the right to reproduce this book or portions thereof in any form whatsoever.

Publisher
10-10-10 Publishing
Markham, ON   Canada

Printed in Canada and the United States of America
First 10-10-10 Publishing paperback edition

Table of Contents

Dedication	v
Foreword	vii
Acknowledgments	ix
Chapter 1: Setting the Stage	1
Chapter 2: Branding - It's More Than a Logo	17
Chapter 3: The Mountain Top vs the Climb – Mission/Vision Statements	29
Chapter 4: Rallying Your Team Behind Your Leadership	41
Chapter 5: Sales and Customer Service – One and the Same	51
Chapter 6: Intro to Marketing – Hard Marketing	61
Chapter 7: Intro to Marketing – Digital Marketing	73
Chapter 8: Financials – The Dreaded Money Chapter	89
Chapter 9: Putting It All Together	101
Chapter 10: Finding Motivation – Time to Take Action	111

This book is dedicated to those in healthcare who really want to see change in the system: change in the way patients are treated, change to the status quo that is private healthcare, and change as an individual.

This book was written in 2020, during the Covid-19 pandemic. This book is also dedicated to all the healthcare workers who treated and cared for those who were in need during this time. You put your lives at risk in order to help others. Thank you.

Foreword

As a healthcare professional, you have something special inside you. You have a gift to offer those patients that need your services. You are an expert in that regard. Now it's time for you to become an expert in running your business and developing yourself as such. *Unf*cking Private Healthcare,* by Daniel Tribby, is a playbook you can use to develop the knowledge, talent, and abilities it takes to run your dream practice and offer an amazing work environment for your team, and an equally amazing experience for your patients.

Daniel's joy and desire to help you become a better business owner is second to none. In this book, he goes deep into business aspects like leadership, sales, marketing, and customer service, which you can use and apply with ease to truly set yourself apart from others in your immediate area. All of the skills and developmental aspects he discusses are necessary traits for you to develop, as a successful business owner.

You hold in your hands a map to personal and professional success. Read it. Learn it. Take action. And watch your business soar!

Raymond Aaron
New York Times Bestselling Author

Acknowledgments

First and foremost, I'd like to thank **Raymond Aaron and the Raymond Aaron Group** for inspiring me to finally write this book. I had been toying with the idea of writing a book for quite some time but wasn't sure how to get it started, nor was I sure about all of the aspects of getting it published. The 10-10-10 program really brought ease and security around how to write this book. You made the process simple and guided me the entire way.

To my wife and business partner, **Pallavi Cherukupally, MD,** Regenerative Sport, Spine, & Spa would not be a reality without your drive to provide excellent care for our patients, and to change the status quo of a society so driven by surgery and medicine. Without this business venture, I would've never been afforded the opportunity to write this book and learn all the things necessary to create change in healthcare and in myself as a business owner. It's been amazing to watch our practice grow and take on this journey with you. It certainly hasn't been easy at times; however, I'm grateful for you and the many trials and tribulations along the way.

To my team at Regenerative Sport, Spine, & Spa, you guys have been amazing to work with. The success of the practice is largely a result of you guys taking massive action and having confidence in us as owners to deliver extraordinary outcomes. I can't thank you enough for your commitments. While at times I certainly wasn't the savviest of business owners or leaders, I appreciate you all helping me through the daily adventures. May the HR Nightmares journal live on forever. **Briana McCormick, Amy Hoffman, Denise Fosgreen, Courtney Allison, Laura Espinosa, Marcela Mayorga.**

Unf*cking Private Healthcare

To **Ian Kornbluth and Tyler Joyce**, founders of Activcore Physical Therapy, who brought me back into healthcare after I swore I would never be a healthcare provider again. Their desire to provide a model that speaks to the needs of the patient rather than be dictated by the limits of insurance were in direct alignment with my beliefs. I have been fortunate to work with you and learn from you. **RJ Donnelly, Haley Conboy, Jacopo Leonardi, Jamie Kornbluth, Dean Hasse, The Princeton Team, Danielle Reid and your Atlanta Team, Ed Foresman and your Colorado Team, Jennifer Joyce, Diane Santarpia and your Billing Team, Ashlea Lyttle, Rob and Ali Liedtka, Michelle Gorton-Boss.**

To the staff at Georgia College & State University Athletic Training department; Head Athletic Trainer, **Paul Higgs**; former Director, **Bud Cooper**; and other associate professors like **Dr. Mike Martino**; thank you for taking so much pride in what you do as educators. You truly raise the bar in the minds of those you educate. I learned countless lessons from each of you, and you were the basis for the foundation of my journey in healthcare.

To my group of friends, there is a saying: "You're only as good as the company you keep." Well, in that case, we all may be screwed! **Kevin Dunn**, you are the definition of a friend. Even when I screwed up royally, you still showed up to make sure I followed through and succeeded in becoming a better person. Your friendship of the last 20 years has been a corner stone in my life; although there has been many a morning I woke up, hungover, wondering why. **Chris Harer** and **Stephen Sewell**, you guys have been lifelong support systems. I have been blessed to call you friends, share wins and losses with you, be at your weddings, and watch you guys grow as professionals, and I can't say enough about you as friends. **Danny Peavey**, I had to put you in here to call you out because I know you'll ask for a free book. All kidding aside, thanks for helping to organize the website for the associating business that thrives off all the ideals in this book. More importantly, thanks for countless memories of 90s music, Rockdale

www.thehealthcareplaybook.com

County, and the fact that you owned 2 Dodge Neons.

A special thank you to **Leslie Bryant**, one of the best human beings, supporters, educators, and future teachers of educators I know. You have been an amazing sounding board for finding proper words, text, punctuation, ideas, and overall editing during this process. They say no single person ever writes a book. Thank you for all you did to help during the process of writing this book.

To **Dee Greene**, your introduction into the social media world for business growth was instrumental in my education of digital marketing. You taught me that social media can be more than just senseless pictures and videos of people without clothes. It can have meaning and draw people to want to know more about your business. You inspired me to learn more, study more, and ultimately drive more business through these channels.

To **Gethro and Trudy Geneus, Dannielle VonDerLinden, and LaTanya Benjamin**—the members of my professional support group—thank you all for your honest feedback and amazing support. I'm blessed to be a part of the group, know each of you, and be able to rely on you. Thanks for always pushing me to do more and get better as a person and as an author.

To **Success Resources America** for providing such a profound way to learn skills and find drive that no educational system provides. I have learned countless lessons as a Quantum Leap member, met countless people to learn from, and made some really great friends in the process. The change in my business and personal mindset is largely attributed to the programs within Success Resources America.

To the countless authors of remarkable books with incredible lessons that have taken me from who I was to who I am becoming as a professional and as a person. Grant Cardone, Robert T. Kiyosaki, Simon Sinek, Napoleon Hill, Mike Michalowicz, T. Harv Eker, Raymond Aaron,

Unf*cking Private Healthcare

Russell Brunson, Tony Robbins, Dean Graziosi, Donald Miller, Angela Duckworth, Gary Vaynerchuk, Daniel Goleman, George Clason, John Mattone, Chris Voss, Marcia Brown, Shelle Rose Charvet, Daymond John, and countless others. Thank you for adding so much value and for sharing your experiences and knowledge.

Lastly, and certainly not least, to my family for their continued support while I was taking the hours necessary to put this book together. Your tolerance of the early morning alarms, the late nights, and weekend work hours were truly a testament to what you guys put up with. To my son, **Rylan Tribby**, you are definitely a large part of my WHY. I hope this book inspires you to do great things and to always put determination and hard work into everything you do. If you want it, go get it. You are the only thing that can stop your success. To my older brother, **Jimmy Jones**, after missing much of our lives together, I can't tell you how much I've appreciated the last 10 years of building our relationship and developing that brotherly bond. To my mom, **Sherry Tribby**, I can't thank you enough for the life experiences you have taught me, and for the undying support you always give me, even during tough conversations that are, at times, hard to hear. To my grandparents, **Daniel Tribby and Dorothy Tribby,** who have passed from this world, you are both a testimony to many of the genuine qualities and lessons I will carry with me forever.

Thank you again to all who contributed to this book and who have contributed value to my life. I love you all.

Chapter 1

Setting the Stage

A patient walks into a healthcare office (sounds like the start to a bad joke)—let's call her Mrs. Jones—signs in on a piece of paper stuck to a clipboard, sits down, grabs a magazine from an array of expired piles of them, and begins to read as she waits to be called upon. A glance up around the room reveals some art on the wall—casual, nice looking—CNN playing some political view points on the lobby TV, and a sign with a picture of Dr. Brown that states, "Voted best local area doctor 3 years in a row."

"Mrs. Jones," a voice from behind the sliding glass calls out.

Mrs. Jones makes her way to the front desk.

"Driver's license and insurance card please," the voice behind the desk requests as the phone is pinched between her shoulder and her ear.

Mrs. Jones hands over the requested cards in exchange for a clipboard (or iPad if the office is keeping up with the times) full of documents, to fill out while she waits to be called back for her appointment.

Twenty minutes go by. Then another 20 minutes. Eventually, the mysterious door that leads to the back office opens up, with a medical assistant standing there, head down, to call out, "Mrs. Jones?"

Unf*cking Private Healthcare

Mrs. Jones is led back through the hallway to a room where she would wait another 20 minutes for the doctor to come in, which is now more than an hour past her appointment time. He would then talk to her for a 5 whole minutes, hand her a prescription, and then escort her back up to schedule a follow-up. That exchange typically looks something like this:

"Mrs. Jones? Hi, I'm Dr. Brown. What brings you in the office today?"

"Well, I have been experiencing some headaches off and on for the last several weeks, which seem to come out of nowhere," she states with a concerned look.

"Uh huh," Dr. Brown mumbles while typing on a laptop computer, not making eye contact. "And have you changed anything recently? Your diet, exercise habits, detergents?"

"No. Everything is the same."

After a few pokes and probes and a range of motion test to her neck, Dr. Brown states, "Well, I don't see anything abnormal. Let's try this prescription for a few weeks and then we will see you back in here. Head back up to the check-out desk and they'll get you taken care of."

Seems like a regular day at a doctor's office, doesn't it? Let me point out a few things to those of you who are thinking, "OK. And?"

1. Do we know anyone's name that works at this practice?

2. Was there any consideration for Mrs. Jones as a person, or what the headaches may be keeping her from accomplishing on a daily basis?

3. Was there any consideration of her time?

www.thehealthcareplaybook.com

4. Was there eye contact and a welcome from the staff?

5. Do we have any idea what this practice has to offer its patients outside of the fact that Dr. Brown has been voted best doctor 3 years in a row?

If you read Mrs. Jones' experience and didn't notice a problem with any of it, then this book is going to open up your eyes to several problems. For those of you that noticed an issue with this, there may be hope for you after all! Either way, the question that I have for you is, "Are you willing to question the status quo?"

Unfortunately, Mrs. Jones' experience has become private healthcare in the United States. Now, I know what most of you are thinking thus far as a healthcare provider or perhaps someone who works in a healthcare office, and it sounds something like this: "Blah, blah, blah, excuse, another excuse, insurance companies, blah, blah, blah."

And my response is this: Let's stop with the bullshit. First, put yourself in the shoes of the consumer. What would you want your experience to look like and feel like at a healthcare office? Every other successful business out there—be it Apple, GM, a pest control company, a bank, or Southwest Airlines—prides itself on loyalty to its customers and the culture of its employees. Why shouldn't healthcare offices?

So how do you create raving fans, marketing that brings people into your practice, and sales tactics that convert; and most importantly, how do you leave Mrs. Jones with a lasting impression of positivity? That's exactly what we're going to discover in this book.

I have found that the majority of healthcare practitioners are one skill away from truly being the best provider or business owner that they can be. That skill usually has nothing to do with their medical profession. Rather, it has to do with learning some of the skills I'm going to present to you in this book. Think about this: How many of

Unf*cking Private Healthcare

you reading this went to success school? Business school? Finance school? Customer service school? Took sales and marketing classes as a part of your medical training? As healthcare providers, most of us are really good at being the provider in our niche; however, the education system failed to give us the extra pieces we need in order to run a successful business.

We will definitely need to start with an honest conversation about where your practice is at this point. What do your online reviews look like? Do you have a power team in place? Do you have a vision and mission statement that your team rallies around? What is the culture like in your practice? Do you have adequate sales funnels in place? Does your marketing speak directly to the person you're trying to attract?

When I mentioned sales, how many of you thought, "What the hell is he talking about? I'm not in sales!" Key point to remember here: Everyone is in sales. It doesn't matter if you sell a product or a treatment plan to a patient; you are in sales. And believe me, it is much harder to sell yourself and a treatment plan than a product. I'm not talking about the pushy, cheesy used car salesman type of sales. I'm talking about how your lobby can sell for you, how your staff can sell for you, and how call to actions actually work in healthcare. These are all topics I will touch on in this book. Most of you don't even realize that your lobby is the perfect place to sell your ancillary services to your patients, and most of you are not using it as such. If you have a service in your practice that can help change the life of one of your perspective patients or current patients, it is your duty as a healthcare professional to sell that service to them.

After reading this book, you will understand why so much marketing in the healthcare industry does not draw people in. You will understand how to create marketing on digital platforms such as social media and your website, as well as hard marketing materials like mailers, letters to clients, and in-office signage that speaks to your

www.thehealthcareplaybook.com

ideal patient. One of the biggest problems that I see when it comes to marketing is that most healthcare practices talk about their expertise and why they are the best bet when it comes to choosing a physical therapist, primary care doctor, neurologist, OB/GYN, etc. But your ideal customer doesn't give a shit about what you do or how great you perceive yourself to be. They only care about how what you do is going to help them feel better, get back to playing golf, or enjoying time with their kids. Read that last sentence again. Your marketing must speak to your clients' needs.

And lastly, but certainly not least important, is customer service. Customer service is that thing that creates raving fans for your practice. It will be that thing that separates you from every other practice in the immediate area, or maybe that thing that separates you from the guy or gal down the block that has the same specialty you do. But customer service has to begin with the culture of your team. The culture of your team starts with leadership within the practice. Are you hiring the right people? Are you hiring based upon personality and not expertise? Do you understand the goals and aspirations of your team on a professional and personal level? Establishing the answers to these questions will help you build a team that will rally around a common mission and vision that all of your patients will grow to love. After all, you want those raving fans to be another source of sales and marketing for your practice.

As a bonus, I will also touch briefly on finances in this book. Why, you ask? Because the majority of healthcare offices have a 60–70% overhead! Again, how many of you went to money management school? This book will help you learn how to cut down on your expenses, adjust your bank accounts (yes, plural: accounts), and save money for taxes.

We will tie all of this up with a nice bow at the end, with strategic action plans that you can begin implementing immediately. Before we get into the nitty gritty of it all, let me first tell you my "why."

*Unf*cking Private Healthcare*

The first place we will start is with my experiences with bad customer service and bad marketing. We've all been subject to bad customer service, whether it was at the grocery store, a car dealership, or with a "customer service" rep on the phone—we've all been there. We've bit our tongues and gripped a tight fist, thinking, "If this m#$%& son of a @&$*$ doesn't...."

We've all decided to stop doing business with certain products, companies, or services because of bad customer service. So, let me ask you this: Are you so bold to think that because you are a healthcare practitioner, people won't do the same to you? Or is it that you don't care, because people need healthcare, after all.

It's that type of thinking that will hold your practice back from ever truly being a place where people feel compassion. What's your "why?" Why did you get into medicine? And please don't say that it was because you wanted to make money, or because you wanted to help people. Those things are commodities, and if you don't dig deeper into WHY you became a healthcare practitioner, you will be like everyone else in town. I will touch more on the subject of finding your why, later in this book.

My favorite story of bad customer service in healthcare came when I was about 20 years old. I was in college studying sports medicine, and I had been having issues with chronic stress, which led to pneumonia and an array of gut issues and heart palpitations. At the beginning of it all, I went to my primary care doctor, like so many of us do, to go through the motions of blood work, ECGs, cardiac stress tests, upper GI tests, MRIs—the works. It was at my primary care doctor's office when I first felt this lack of caring and compassion.

I was greeted by that familiar sliding glass window and the front office employee that didn't introduce herself or give me the time of day, other than to ask for my driver's license and insurance cards. I waited

www.thehealthcareplaybook.com

almost an hour past my appointment time to see my doctor, and when I did, his suggestion was that maybe I needed to cut some weight and I would feel better. Now, I was an athlete through high school, and I worked out regularly, 4 to 5 days per week. At that time, I stood at 6'2" and carried about 205 pounds, so I was anything but out of shape. I was so flabbergasted at my doctor's response that I offered for him to meet me at the gym later that day.

It's this type of poor service and consideration for what I was going through that really spoke to what that doctor gave a damn about. It clearly was not me and the emotional toll that this change in my health had taken. I find that this type of "care" is still so prevalent in healthcare today.

My favorite part about all of this is that most healthcare practitioners don't realize that their patients are another source of marketing for them as a practitioner. When you do a good job of connecting with peoples' feelings and what they're going through, they become advocates for the care that you provide. This is largely missed in healthcare marketing.

Speaking of the sort, let's segue into poor marketing for medical practices. I've had my fair share of "marketing consultants" that have had zero experience in actually running a healthcare practice. They tend to focus on what we do, and not who we are and who we want to attract. They offer the kind of business that drives me crazy. I call it, "Wouldn't you like to have 30 more leads a month" crap. They went to college to learn marketing from an array of professors who themselves have never owned a business, let alone a medical one, and my ignorance of the sort caused me to spend countless dollars on marketing that did not draw people in. I'm sure many of you reading this can relate. The problem is, again, how many of you went to school to learn how to market? We put our trust in someone who claims to be an "expert" to help us get our message out there, and then when

Unf*cking Private Healthcare

that message doesn't convert, we get frustrated and move on to the next person, who again can't convey the message properly. Rinse and repeat.

I've worked with social media marketers that have used cat memes on our feeds! WTF! Are you kidding me? What does that have to do with inviting people into a conversation about their health? You would be astounded at the answer that I got. It went something like this:

"Well, you can't just put pictures of yourself and your business on your social media feeds all day. People will tune you out. You have to mix it up."

I laughed sarcastically at this comment because how many of you actually pay attention to those memes, or better yet, scroll past them on your feed? Those types of things don't speak to the person you're trying to attract. They only say, "I don't have anything important to tell you today, so I'm going to add some fluff." You become boring and lumped into the category of "another medical office."

At this point, I'm sure you're thinking, "OK, Daniel. I hear what you're saying, but what makes you the opposite of what you just described?" And the answer is simple. My belief is, "the way you've always done it" is where innovation goes to die. We must constantly change our ways of thinking and our ways of dealing with people, in order to continue to provide not only the best care but the best atmosphere for people to feel good about doing business with us.

At this point in my writing, I have been a business owner for the last six years. So what led me to start my own business? I'll tell you.

In early 2013, I had been working for nearly a decade at one of the largest orthopedic practices in the southeast, in their physical rehabilitation department. I was getting frustrated at the quantity over quality type of mentality. We were expected to continue to treat high

www.thehealthcareplaybook.com

volumes of patients while being graded on customer service scores, without consideration for the patient's outcome. These customer service scores would have a direct influence on yearly bonuses that we could make. The problem was that those bonuses were not based upon how great your scores were, but how much you could improve upon them during that given year. In other words, the office that I worked in, which was one of 22 under the same umbrella at the time, held the highest customer service scores in the company, but was offered the lowest percentage of bonuses. (I know what you're thinking: WTF, right?) The office that had the lowest scores, but made the most improvement on those scores, got the highest percentage bonus. Meaning, an office that runs at 98% positive customer service scores, would not make the same bonus as the office that had 75% positive customer service scores, because they improved from 40% to that astounding 75%. (Insert eye roll.) No matter how well we did, the feeling was always, "Well, this is great; how much more can you do?"

This ultimately led me to believe that the modern healthcare system was garbage. Looking back on it, I can see that this is where I first wanted to see changes made in the healthcare system. Not just because I was an employee of that system, but because the consumers in that system deserved a better experience. This became my WHY.

After leaving that group, I decided that I needed to explore different occupational opportunities that would allow me to grow as a person, both professionally and personally. I started working for a small medical sales company and had some early success, which led me to being a regional sales director for that company. What I began to realize was that sales is something that is important in every industry. Selling a product or service didn't matter. Products are easy; services—total different story. If you think for one second as a healthcare provider that you're not in sales, you are completely misled.

The knowledge I gained from working in the medical sales industry led me to start my own medical sales company. I specialized in surgical hardware as well as regenerative medicine products. I was having so much fun working for myself, making money I would have never made as a "rehab guy," and learning all these new tools to make my business successful. I starting thinking to myself that I would never go back to being a provider of healthcare services. I swore it! But never say never.

Fast forward to 2017. I had an opportunity to open up a brand new practice that centered on natural healing through regenerative medicine, stem cell therapy, and physical rehabilitation. Sounds like a home run, right? One of the doctors that I worked with at the prior practice I mentioned, had similar aspirations and beliefs around how medicine should be delivered. We packed up our shit and moved from Atlanta to Orlando to start this venture. I learned very quickly what it meant to own a medical practice. And believe me, you don't know what you don't know. We struggled with finding the proper marketing, how to sell our services in this new market, how to find a power team, and most importantly, how to lead our team and develop a culture that would speak to our patients. Feeling that "in over your head" sensation is quite sobering. I'm sure many of you can relate.

We knew that if this practice was going to survive, we were going to have to change a model that had been so ingrained in us from working in that other, larger practice. I began going to seminars, reading books, studying social media, learning website content, attending leadership courses, plowing through customer service books, and studying branding. And guess what? It began to pay off. We saw our business double in revenue from year one to year two. People began to ask me, "How have you guys been so successful so early? What is it that you're doing?"

And thus, the beginning of this book.

Let me assure you that I have made every mistake possible in running a healthcare business; I have made poor marketing decisions, I've been a bad leader, I've spent unnecessary money, and I've served my

www.thehealthcareplaybook.com

clients at a level less than they deserve, as well as my team. It's the recognition of this that has made the difference. I know I will never be perfect at everything, nor will you, but the pursuit of perfection is what inspires me (and it should you) to keep learning more and keep sharing more. It's what inspires every good business owner out there.

In the coming chapters of this book, I will share with you those things I have learned, in hopes that it will also help you become a better business owner, a better practitioner, and a more reliable resource for your team. We're going to dive deep into aspects like leadership, your mission and vision, your why, customer service, sales and marketing, and an array of other tips and tricks that will transform the look and feel of your practice. Gone will be the days where your marketing sucks and your team just punches a clock for a paycheck. Sound too good to be true? It just might be if you're unwilling to have an honest discussion with yourself about the state of your practice and state of your mindset.

As mentioned in the title, this book is for private healthcare practices and the employees of the those practices who wish to improve their offerings to their patients, have a greater work/life balance, create a workplace that people enjoy being a part of, and generate more revenue. If that sounds like you, GREAT! It matters not if you're a physical therapy practice, primary care doctor, a specialist MD, OB/GYN, DC, ABC, DEF, or XYZ.... You get my point... the skills will apply.

There are a few things I require before I will work with anyone personally on developing themselves and their practice:

1. As mentioned, you must be a private practice. If you have multiple providers, that's okay too. Multiple locations, no worries.

2. You are not willing to accept the status quo, and you have a big dream for your practice. Big dreams and high expectations of yourself will give you the tenacity to build your practice.

Unf*cking Private Healthcare

3. You must be able to have tough conversations about the topics in this book, even if the reality check hurts your feelings. Self-reflection is the only thing that propels you forward.

4. Your work ethic has to be there. If you've read Grant Cardone's 10x Rule, then you know what I'm talking about. After all, what good is money spent if you're not going to implement?

5. You must have ethics. I will not work with shady ass medical providers who do illegal stuff and cut corners to get ahead.

Now, I believe it's also important to address who this book is NOT for. This book is not for hospital systems and large corporate medical entities who solely focus on productivity over customer experience and staff satisfaction. Also, if you have a history of collecting knowledge and neglecting the action part, this book is probably not for you. Lastly, if you're in a business partnership and you're all in, but your partner tends to be Negative Nancy, this probably isn't for you either.

I believe in small businesses and, as a small business owner, my desire is to help you succeed as such. I believe personal development, grit, and tenacity to be qualities of people who succeed in building the practice they have dreamed about. Again, if this is you, then let's get started!

Let's have a gut-check moment right now. This part is definitely my second favorite, the first being after the change that happens; however, change can't happen until you can identify the issues, come to grips with them, and take massive action in changing them. Nothing—I repeat, nothing—happens without massive action.

As we move toward the end of this chapter, I want you to take a real, honest look at your practice. There will be some tough questions you will need to answer, and sometimes those answers come with

www.thehealthcareplaybook.com

realizations of things we need to change. Some of those changes may be easy. For instance, changing the way the lobby is set up, or starting an email marketing campaign. But some are going to be difficult. Maybe you need to make a change on your team, or maybe you need to realize that the culture in your office is the direct reflection of poor leadership, which ultimately falls on you. Either way, identifying those things is the first step.

Let's get to it. I am going to list out 5 separate categories, with some questions that I want you to write down the answers to. I will give you some guidelines to follow; but again, be honest with yourself. If you're having a hard time deciding if you're fluffing your answer or not, just ask one of your team members. Why, you ask? Because patients see you as a provider, and your team knows you as a person and a leader. They see the good, the bad, and the ugly. Remember that little piece I just gave you, when we get to the leadership portion of this book.

1. Do you have a vision and mission statement? If you do, which I find to be rare in most healthcare offices, who does it speak to? Is your vision the change you want to see in the world, or just the vision you have for yourself? Does everyone on your team know your mission? Can they recite it? Are they rallied behind it?

2. How's the culture of your team? Are they excited to be part of your practice, and conspire to deliver great service to your patients? Have you had regular individual meetings with each one of them to talk about their personal and professional goals? Do they come to work because they believe in you as their leader, or because they need a paycheck? Do you have someone on your team that sours the culture? Do you need to make the decision to coach that person up or coach them out?

3. How is your marketing working? Do you have a sound digital marketing playbook that includes emails, social media, your website, a YouTube Channel, or podcast? Does your hard

Unf*cking Private Healthcare

marketing material attract people to what you offer when they're sitting in your lobby? Or are you distracting people in your lobby with magazines and CNN? Are you getting leads from your marketing efforts? Do people even know you exist?

4. How are your customer reviews—4 stars? 5? 3.2? Are you good at capturing them and getting them on digital platforms such as Google or Facebook? Maybe you have a written testimonials book in your lobby. Have you gotten any video testimonials that you have shared in an email campaign?

5. Lastly, what is the financial situation of your practice? Do you find yourself wondering at times if you're going to make payroll this week? Do you find yourself spending money on equipment that you didn't have to spend? During tax season, are you nervous about how much money you're going to have to pay out, because it's not available? Are you paying yourself first? Do you have multiple bank accounts for the practice so that you can adequately budget? Are you caught up in trying to manage your own spreadsheets?

I hope you took serious time to consider those five aspects of your practice, and that you were truly honest with yourself. Like most practices, I have no doubt that there are multiple things that you are really good at. On the other hand, I'm quite sure there are things that could use some improvement. I find the number one thing that needs to be improved is the culture of your team. And the best way to do this is to establish a mission for your team that everyone can rally around. However (and here's another gut check), you as the leader, owner, or manager are responsible for being the face of it. It's your duty to pay attention to it and give 100% to it, even on days when you don't feel like it. After all, if you aren't doing it, why should they?

www.thehealthcareplaybook.com

In the next chapter, we are going to start putting pieces together that will help you with your mission and vision statements. In order to write those statements and get your team rallied behind them, you must first discover the essence of your brand.

Chapter 2

Branding – It's More Than a Logo

"But Trib (this is the nickname most people professionally know me as), I already have a logo and a name. I don't need to talk about my brand; I have that. I thought this book was about sales and marketing and customer service."

Let me clear this part up for you. Yes, the main focus is on sales, marketing, and customer service; however, in order to get the right message out there, and in order to teach your team how to convey that message the right way, you have to start with discovering what that right message is. Any asshole can show you how to put some stuff on social media and in an email campaign. I want to show you how to put together something that sticks in the market place. Something that makes you stand out. In order to do that, we have to start with your WHY. Oh, and by the way, your "brand" is much more than a logo and fancy letters on your business card. If you think otherwise, you're sadly mistaken.

Let me give you an example of this: If you need to blow your nose, you reach for a "Kleenex," right? Kleenex is a brand; tissue is the product. If you live in the south, everything is a "Coke." It doesn't matter if it's a Sprite, Dr. Pepper, or an orange soda; it is still considered a "Coke." Again, Coke is the brand, and the product is a soda. These companies' brands have become the product, and vice versa. When you want to look something up on the internet, how many of you say "Google it?" Google is just one search engine, but they've created

Unf*cking Private Healthcare

synergy between their brand and a product. If product companies can do it, why can't service companies? Why can't your healthcare office do it in your immediate area? Hasn't famous orthopedist, Dr. Andrews, done exactly that? Just because he has branded himself in this way, does that make him more qualified to do the same shoulder surgery that any other orthopedist could perform? Absolutely not, but what it has done is make him a staple in the sports community, to where every athlete who is injured will seek out the advice of someone at the Andrews Institute.

This is what is referred to as existing in the "me only" space. Let me explain. So many healthcare offices don't separate themselves from other like-offices. There could be 10 different neurologists in any given city, and they all do the same damn thing! Why do we choose one over another one? The answers range from, "I like the feel of their office," to "I like their staff," or "The doctor is nice." Ultimately, the educational level is the same, so why would it matter which office any particular patient went to. This should be really obvious to you. It's about the people that work in the office. It's the experience people have when they walk in your doors. They may even say, "It's the only office where I feel like a person and not a number on a page," or "They're better about timeliness. I don't have to wait 17 hours to be seen."

Some of you exist in the "me too" space—meaning, you're not special. You blend in with all other offices. You're not memorable. You don't lead with why you're in business; therefore, you get grouped into the category of "every other office." Think about it; Dr. Andrews has staked claim as the leading orthopedist for athletes. This is "me only" space. What is the reputation of your office in the immediate area? What do you specialize in? Don't tell me you specialize in neurology either! Tell me that your office is the only neurologist that inspires hope for those with MS. Tell me your regenerative medicine center is the only office where people can go for cutting edge nonsurgical treatment that gives

www.thehealthcareplaybook.com

them their youth back. Start thinking in terms of how people will feel when they do business with you.

In order to separate yourself and step into that "me only space," like these other companies and individuals have, you first have to clarify your message. In Simon Sinek's book, Start with Why, he repeats over and over this simple phrase: "People don't buy what you do. They buy why you do it." Knowing there is so much truth to this is the reason you need to start with why. Too often, I see healthcare practices talk about 2 main things: what they do and why they are the best at it.

What you do, often looks like this: "We take care of your back pain by getting to the root cause of it." (Insert the eye roll emoji here.) The problem with this sentence is that no one knows what the hell it means! My follow-up question to this statement is usually, "Oh yeah, how do you do that?" The answer is inevitably some technical-based answer that is full of medical jargon. As a provider, I understand the jargon; however, if you're willing to explain yourself to me that way, you're most likely doing the same with your patients, and they will have zero clue what the hell you're talking about.

The second part of your messaging problem I mentioned, is the "why you are the best at it" part. I see this phraseology a lot: "When it comes to physical therapy, we're your best bet." (Palm to face on this one.)

These statements don't speak to the patient's needs. You know why? Because you haven't talked to them yet. You've only talked about what you do and how great you are. Spoiler alert: No one cares if you're the top cardiologist in the great state of Indiana, if you're a dick. People do business with people they like, and people do business with people who talk directly to them about how to solve their problems. Think back to the opening chapter about Dr. Brown addressing Mrs. Jones with his attention buried into a laptop.

*Unf*cking Private Healthcare*

Your messaging has to include some key components. You must take your potential patient on a journey that shows them what it will be like to do business with you. First, you must address a problem. That problem is not their medical issue. It's the thing the medical issue keeps them from doing. For example, back pain could be the medical issue; however, it is also back pain that keeps you from working, rendering you unable to provide for your family... now, that's a true problem. This is the spot where your empathy needs to shine through in your messaging. You have to show people that you understand how frustrating, heartbreaking, or depressing their particular situation can be.

Secondly, you must address how you solve the problem. This is where you can show your authority. The rule is, you are not allowed to show your authority until you have shown empathy for the person you are speaking to and their particular problem. Here is how it works.

"We understand how nervous and unprepared you may feel as a first-time mother. That's why our team of OB/GYNs are committed to spending 30 minutes of 1-on-1 time with you during your first visit, to make sure you get all your questions answered."

In that statement, you have addressed a problem that first-time mothers may be feeling. Again, "feeling." You're pulling at the heart strings here. You have shown authority by saying that they will see an actual doctor (OB/GYN), not a PA, and they will get 30 minutes of 1-on-1 time. No one else out there in their immediate area may be doing that. This helps them feel more at ease and cared for when they come to your office. And you have potentially established yourself as the only OB/GYN office that offers a 30-minute initial visit. Remember that "me only" thing I mentioned earlier?

And lastly, you must provide a clear way of doing business with you: Call to schedule; click here to request an appointment. Sounds pretty obvious, right? You would be surprised how many healthcare offices

www.thehealthcareplaybook.com

don't have super clear instructions on their website about how to schedule and what that process looks like. If this isn't you, and you have multiple clear calls to action on your website, great job; however, the younger generations do most of their business on social media. Do you have links to appointment scheduling platforms on your social media? (There is more on social media marketing, in Chapter 7.)

Let's get technical, medical, and scientific for a second. Two major centers of your brain, the neocortex and the limbic system, are responsible for how you make decisions. The neocortex is that analytical part of your brain that allows you to make very calculated decisions. It feels no emotion. The limbic system, on the other hand, is the part of the brain that is creative and artsy and emotional. Take a guess as to which system you want to target in people's decisions about doing business with you? Your messaging needs to target the limbic system. The limbic system is that "gut feeling" system that a lot of people rely on. Think about it; was there ever a time when you thought too hard and made a calculated decision that was the wrong one—you weighed every single option, you made a pros and cons list, you talked to your family, you talked to your friends, and you ended up making the wrong choice? Versus going by that emotional gut feeling that you had, and it ended up being the right one? This is how people make decisions on where to buy. If you appeal to the limbic system in your messaging, you will win.

So, when it comes to messaging and branding, what is that thing you do that no one else is doing? What is it like to do business with you? What separates you from everyone else and keeps you from being grouped into "just another healthcare office?" This is of utmost importance because if you don't brand yourself, someone else will, and it's usually into a group of similar people offering similar stuff, or as mentioned earlier, "me too" space.

A good way to separate yourself from similar offices in your area is to answer the question, "What do you stand for?" I'm not talking about your Hippocratic Oath or any other ethical oath you may have taken in order to become a healthcare provider. I'm talking about how you show people who you are versus what you do. For example, I believe the typical physical therapy offering is a crap system. I'm not saying physical therapists are crap. It's a shame I have to qualify that in today's world. I believe whole heartedly in physical rehabilitation, and I believe it is widely undervalued, but there is a reason for that. That reason is that the majority of the practices in my immediate area (and probably yours) are very high volume practices. They treat large quantities of patients at any given time, overwork their therapists, use too much support staff, and don't offer anything above a factory production type of experience. In fact, if you research the numbers, you will find that less than 10% of people who begin a physical therapy regimen actually complete it. That's astonishing, and quite frankly, unacceptable. The problem is, most physical therapy practices will blame the system and will make changes to coincide with what the system dictates. I personally couldn't tolerate that or accept it as the "way it is," so when I decided to open my physical therapy practice, I decided that our potential patients deserved to feel like more than a number on a page. They would be offered one-on-one treatment for an hour of time. We would not use assistants or aides or any sort of support staff. As a patient, you got the time you deserved with your therapist. It allowed me to say, "We are the only physical therapy office in the area that offers one-hour-long sessions, one-on-one treatment, and the ability for you to be heard." I chose to no longer be part of the status quo. I stood for a better experience for the patient because they deserved it. Also, it showed any physical therapist I hired that I cared about their ability to provide excellent care and use the skills they spent so much time learning.

Let me tell you about the amount of haters that came crawling when I opened that business. "No one will value that. How are you going to get money?" Insurance this and insurance that. Ugh. Small thinkers. I even heard the director of another local physical therapy office that was hospital based say, "Why would it matter if I'm treating more than

www.thehealthcareplaybook.com

one person at a time if you're getting better?" That type of thinking is why you will always be in last place, sir. If you went to a store and the sales person in the store that was helping you was also helping four other people at the same time, how great is that experience going to be for you? Yes, maybe you got what you came for, but are you likely to recommend anybody else go shop there?

I'll ask again: What do you stand for? Are you just feeding into the status quo of every other offering that every other office with the same specialty as yours is doing? Or are you offering people a better experience? Are you offering to make people feel a certain way? Are you standing for something greater?

What you stand for will show people who you are. Remember when I said that people do business with people? People also do business with like-minded people. If you are a mom, people will do business with you just because you're a mom and they can relate to the feeling of being a mom. If you are a beach volleyball player, other people who are athletes or who can relate to beach volleyball will most likely be interested in doing business with you. You're probably thinking, "Well, how would people know that?" Easy. You tell them. We will talk more about this in the chapters ahead on marketing. So, who are you? Do your patients know you as a person or just another healthcare provider? Are you blending in with all the other providers with the same specialty in your area, or are you standing out?

Now that we have discussed what it is you stand for, let's switch gears to identifying who your ideal patient is. Let's do a recap on our offices we have discussed so far. We saw the OB/GYN office that offers more 1-on-1 time with first-time mothers, giving their potential patients a safe and secure place to talk about their concerns. Maybe you are a physical therapy office that only treats 1-on-1, versus the high volume model that's so prevalent in that niche right now. Maybe you pride yourself on supreme customer service in a family environment. Whatever that "thing" is, it must be part of your messaging and

23

Unf*cking Private Healthcare

branding. Once you have this message in place, we then have to identify the audience for whom that message needs to be in front of.

Are you talking to your ideal patient? Where do they live? Where do they hang out? Who do they associate with? And please don't tell me, "Well, Trib, we're for anyone that suffers from chronic pain." If you're for everyone, you're for no one. End of story. You must accurately define your niche in the market place.

In order to discover who your ideal patient is, I have a little exercise for you. Let's group your patients into 3 separate categories. Your first group—let's call them Tier 1—are your raving fans. These people will spend serious dollars at your office. They recommend everyone come see you. They send you referrals. They do testimonials for you. These people think you hung the moon.

Tier 2 are your everyday, run-of-the-mill types of people. They pay the bills. You have a good relationship with them, but they usually don't openly advocate for you. They like you and trust you but wouldn't go out of their way to help you grow.

Lastly, is Tier 3. These are the patients you need to fire. These are the ones that are never satisfied no matter how much you bend over backward for them. They're the complainers—the ones where you look at the schedule, see their name, and say, "shit."

Now, once you have discovered your Tier 1 people, guess what else you just discovered? This is your ideal patient. This is the person you should want to clone over and over again. Tier 2 people will come and go, and these people are good right where they are. And I have no doubt that you have just realized that you need to fire some patients as well. The problem I see the majority of the time, particularly in brand new health care practices, is that they try to satisfy everyone just so they can get money in to pay the bills. While I totally understand that, the problem that you invite into your practice is that

www.thehealthcareplaybook.com

you are not really clear on who it is you serve.

Hopefully, by breaking down your patients into those 3 tiers, you have a clear idea of what you attract and who you want to continue to attract. If you happen to realize you don't really have any Tier 1 type of people, you're definitely in the right place. Keep reading.

Now that you have identified your top tier patient, you need to figure out how to target them. Where are they? In order to do that, you must consider 2 things. What are the demographics and psychographics of this niche? Demographics are things like, are they male or female, or both? How old are they? How much money do they make? Where do they live? Psychographics are what they're interested in. Where do they hang out? With whom do they hang out? What activities do they participate in?

Here's how it works. Let's stick with our OB/GYN. You aren't for all pregnant women; you're for pregnant women between the ages of 30 and 45, who live in the greater Orlando, Florida area, and are looking for a concierge service. Perfect; well, if it's a concierge service, that usually means higher cost to the patient, but it also could mean that the patient gets more access to you as a doctor, gets longer visits, has special times available to them, etc. So, you would want to identify what areas of greater Orlando these women live in. What zip codes yield higher household incomes? Where do they spend their leisure time? Are there local moms groups you could connect with? Do they play golf, tennis, or other country club types of activities? Are they part of boutique fitness studios like Orange Theory or Barre? Are there potentially other physicians within this niche already, that aren't in your specialty but who could become a referral source? This is where big thinking comes into play. This is where healthcare offices truly start to separate themselves from other offices, because they have defined who their niche is and where to find them. They begin concentrating their marketing efforts to these groups, specifically and ultimately cloning their Tier 1 patients. They don't send out mailers across the

Unf*cking Private Healthcare

entire state. They don't market to anyone and everyone. They target their niche specifically.

Here is the best part of defining your niche and who you are for. When you do this, you also define who you are not for. Remember at the beginning of this book when I identified who the book is not for? In my own personal practice, I have also identified who my services are not for. This makes decision making very easy. There are many times that people will call the office, and their values don't align with my offerings. No problem. I very politely tell them that this is not the office for them, and I refer them to somebody else who is in their wheelhouse. This is a beautiful, magical thing that cuts the bullshit out of my practice, keeps my staff from having to deal with it, and ultimately keeps the stress of that Tier 3 group out of my life. If I am cloning my Tier 1 people, then I am perfectly matching up my services with their desires. When I start inviting the other junk in, it causes more stress for me and my team. When you have identified your niche, who your services are for, and your team has rallied behind it, you will be surprised as to how powerfully your team will show up, because they understand exactly who it is they are there to serve. They feel empowered to service that particular patient, and they also feel empowered to tell people that don't fit that niche that this isn't the practice for them. Think about Southwest Airlines, who values its employees before its customers. Southwest doesn't believe that the customer is always right. Southwest has determined that it will not accept poor behavior toward its employees. They have identified who they are for and what they will not tolerate. Think about how powerful that culture must be. Imagine if your team came to work every day with a clear sense of who they serve, and with confidence that their leader, you, is going to stand up for them in the face of anyone who mistreats them.

Once you have discovered your new messaging and what you stand for, and have identified your top tier patient type, and the demographics and psychographics of where they are, you have one

26

www.thehealthcareplaybook.com

more step to take. You must show people the process of doing business with you. This is particularly important for medical practices because everything you offer is intangible. Imagine if I wanted to open a bakery. I could start making cakes, pies, and cookies, and offering free samples to the friends of people in my neighborhood or my family, and gauge their feedback as to how good my baked goods are. Cakes, cookies, and pies are tangible things. I can touch them, taste them, smell them, etc. But how does someone sample your medical office? Offer a sample shoulder injection just to see how they do? Can you have a practice run at delivering a baby?

"Hey, Mrs. Jones, pop this pill real quick and let's see how you like it."

It's tough to do because healthcare services are not tangible. You have to pay to play. There are no free samples. How do we make the intangible, feel tangible to our potential patients? Again, we tell them. We give them a description of exactly what it looks like to do business with us.

I have included a portion of the chart that shows you the process we use at our regenerative medicine center. You can also find a print-ready version of this chart, at www.thehealthcareplaybook.com/booktools.

Steps	What Happens	Value	Outcome
Engage/Discover	Phone call or walk in	Builds rapport, establishes trust. Most people have a low expectation of the service they receive; we want to build relationships with our patients.	We've established enough rapport and have built a comfort level that converts the patient into a scheduled appointment.
Private Consult	1 on 1 30 min with MD	Patients get the time they deserve to discuss their goals and to voice their feelings.	Together, the MD and the patient come up with a treatment plan that satisfies the patient's goals
Treatment Plan	Elected procedure	Mode of natural healing and pain relief without the use of surgery or pain medications.	You begin your journey of feeling youthful again.

Unf*cking Private Healthcare

This chart shows a step-by-step process that we walk our potential patients through from their first interaction with us. It starts with the initial introduction, be it a phone call or walk in, takes them through their initial consultation, and finally their procedure if they have one. What you will notice about this chart is that while it does mention the "what," it is more focused on the "why." You want people to see the value of each of these steps, and to realize what it is that they are going to get, and what it is they will feel during each step. I have mentioned this multiple times already: People don't care what you do. They only care about how what you do is going to help them.

After you have identified the steps, you will then need to train your staff on how to present the steps to your patients when they call or walk in. You will also need to translate this to a value stack on your website. How, you ask? We will touch on these items in other chapters.

Action time! Take the time to actually fill this chart out. Think deeply about what steps every patient takes when doing business with you and what their outcome should be. What are they going to feel? Why is that important for their success and yours? You can have more than 3 steps, but I would not go more than 4. Think about it like this: Every time you offer someone a piece of information, you are handing them a 10 lb. dumbbell. How many of those dumbbells could you hand someone before they drop them and say, "The hell with this. It's too complicated." Keep the message clear and concise.

Okay, there was lots of information in this chapter. Hopefully, you took some time to write things down and create action items for yourself. This chapter is a huge building block for the next chapters. You cannot adequately market or sell your services if you don't know the why behind your how, what, and who. You cannot create a power team without identifying what you stand for. And furthermore, you won't be able to create your vision and mission statements that become the corner stone of your business and the basis for motivation of your team. This is what we're going to talk about in the next chapter.

Chapter 3

The Mountain Top vs the Climb – Mission/Vision Statements

When you first had the thought of owning your own private healthcare practice, many of you may have wrote down a vision and mission for your practice. You had to put together a business plan and present it to whatever investment group that was going to fund your adventure, along with all the financials that you would end up not even coming close to meeting. But you were motivated and excited about being a business owner and a practitioner under your own terms, having your own team, your own brick and mortar space, your own rules, etc. You thought of all the wonderful ways you were going to help people, and how different your practice was going to be. You considered the friendships you would build with your staff, and the way you would be viewed by your family and in your community. Then reality set in and you realized you didn't know what you didn't know about owning your own practice. You didn't realize all of the pieces that you would need in order to be successful. You didn't realize the insane amount of work that it would take to get everyone rallied around a common goal. And your vision and mission, much like those early financials, ended up tucked away in a dusty file drawer.

Believe me, I know. That was exactly what happened to me. Remember when I told you I have already made all these mistakes? I have been a bad leader, business owner, terrible marketer, sales person, etc. I had no idea where I wanted to go or how to get there. My team lost confidence in me, and money was dwindling. I had

Unf*cking Private Healthcare

forgotten why I started my practice. It was only after taking the time to identify what my vision and mission were, that I was able to start the process of putting the pieces back together.

Maybe that last paragraph describes you. Perhaps your vision and mission have changed since you first had the thought of opening your doors. Maybe you never even had one to begin with. And I'd be willing to bet a fair amount of money that the majority of you reading this book have zero idea if your staff even knows what those vision and mission statements are. And then there is a small percentage of you who think it doesn't matter and that I'm full of shit—you're in my Tier 3 group—and as mentioned before, this book probably isn't for you. But for those of you in my Tier 1 and Tier 2 groups, let's get on with it.

I want you to think about this question as we move through this chapter: Why are your patients your patients, and why are your employees your employees?

If your answer to this question is, "I'm not sure," or some other arbitrary answer such as, "Because we're good at what we do," then hopefully this chapter will provide some clarity around your answer. Or perhaps it will provide clarity around what you aren't doing well and how you need to fix it. Or my personal favorite realization: "Damn. I'm a shittier business owner then I thought." And that's okay! The simple realization of that makes you more likely to change. Again, you don't know what you don't know, so let's build the confidence in yourself and your team, to new levels!

Before we get to the art of actually writing these statements, let's talk about why they are important. A lot of you may be thinking that vision and mission statements are typically for larger companies or larger corporations, but I'm going to tell you that vision and mission statements are the essence of what you stand for and what your team can rally behind. It makes no difference if you're a team of three people or a company of 300,000 people. These statements are the

www.thehealthcareplaybook.com

change you want to see in the world. They are the actions that you and your team put into place that define who you are as a company. One is the mountain top, and the other is the climb to get to the mountain top. One is part of your why, and the other is the how and the what. They both breed loyalty of your patients and your team. They both define your purpose.

Your purpose; here's a big thing: What is your purpose? Please don't tell me that it is to help people and make money. No shit. I get that much. I'm talking about why you chose to open your own office. What's at the core of who you are? What do you see or want to see in the future? And even more importantly, what does your staff see in you? What do they want for their future? Are they rallied around your purpose because it falls in line with their own? We will touch more on your staff in the next chapter, and how to get them to rally around that purpose.

Let's start with identifying your vision. The vision is your mountain top. It's the change you want to see in the world. According to computerhistory.org, Bill Gates, owner of Microsoft, guided by a belief that the computer would be a valuable tool on every office desktop and in every home, began developing software for personal computers. You see, Bill Gates didn't develop his company so that he could be a billionaire. That wasn't the drive behind what he started. He believed that every office and home in America would have a computer for personal use, in a time when computers were exclusively for larger companies, factories, and corporations.

The vision at our regenerative medicine practice is that surgery will no longer be touted as the best option for spine and joint problems, and using addictive pain medicine will be a thing of the past.

These statements have nothing to do with us as people or our own personal gain. They have everything to do with who we want to serve and the change we want to see. I see so many people put their own

Unf*cking Private Healthcare

personal growth and gain in their vision statements. It's fine if you have your own personal goals, but they don't belong as part of the vision statement for your healthcare practice. Think about it like this: How likely is your team to get behind making you the top cardiologist in New York City, versus the vision to decrease heart disease in America? See the difference? Your vision should not be about your own gain; rather, about a higher purpose that changes the economy for the better, or health for the better, or the world for the better. It's one sentence and it's a big, big goal. Make it nearly unreasonable. Make it almost out of reach so that it inspires you daily to try and reach for it.

So ask yourself: What is that big change you want to make happen in the world? What is your mountaintop? If you could pick one major thing that could have a direct effect on the world, what would it be? Just make sure that vision is relatable to what you actually do. For instance, if you are a cardiologist, your vision would not be to abolish knee pain. Be very specific. If you're on OB/GYN, your vision should not be, "Changing the face of women's healthcare." What about women's healthcare do you want to change?

Let's do a few more examples of vision statements so that you get the idea.

1. Pain management physician: "Our vision is to eliminate the overuse of pain medicine in the United States.

2. Physical therapy group: "Our vision is that medicine and surgery will stop being the norm, and physical therapy will emerge as the leading first step for helping people in pain.

3. OB/GYN: "Our vision is that every woman will realize that the benefits of our physician services go well beyond pregnancy and menstruation management."

www.thehealthcareplaybook.com

4. The vision for this book is that it starts the process of propelling me to the number 1 business coach for private healthcare.

Do you see what these statements do? They subtly present an underlying problem and a change that you as a provider could influence. And they are big dreams and changes. The bigger, the better, and the more you will strive to reach for them.

Also, notice that they describe a change in the vision of the patient you are trying to attract. Your patient's vision is equally as important. What do they want? Do you know? You're thinking, "Trib, how the hell do you find that out?" Simple; ask. How many of you as providers have actually taken the time to ask your patients what they want when they come to your office? We often think they are there because they need our particular services. While this is true, what else might they be expecting? These are questions you need to ask yourself. In fact, they are questions you should ask of the patients who are no longer your patients, because they are the ones that you didn't serve. They are the patients that have found another place that speaks to what their vision is.

You need to realize that the expectations a typical patient has for how they will be treated are extremely low when they enter into a healthcare office. People expect to have long wait times, to be ignored by the majority of the staff, to be escorted back and forth, and not to have all their questions answered. The list goes on and on. This is the dynamic that has been created within "modern" healthcare in the United States. Most of you will blame that on insurance companies, but insurance companies have only changed their reimbursement. Do you know what they haven't changed? Natural human interaction. Courtesy. Manners. Politeness. Care. Concern. It takes a very small shift to change that dynamic, and the offices that do, are the ones that you have lost patients to.

Unf*cking Private Healthcare

Your vision for the change you want to see should align with the vision your Tier 1 clients are looking for. Be sure to take your client's vision into consideration when you're writing your own. When these two align, you will have synergy in your goals, synergy in your team, and synergy between you and your patient. At this point, you will begin to put the little pieces into place that will help you accomplish that vision. It's the steps you take to climb the mountain that become your mission.

Your mission is the "how to" for your vision. It is the path that you take to your vision. It is all the little intricacies you and your team do together to ensure your vision is met. The mission is what rallies your team around common goals. It should compel you to act on the vision. So, how do you build a mission statement?

First, let's identify the what, then the how. The "what" are the actionable things you do that make a difference. What do you offer that no one else does? What is your expertise? What is the one thing or set of things that people can only get if they come to you? Again, this is creating that "me only" type of space for yourself. If you forgot what "me only" means, go back to Chapter 2 now.

What you offer has to go deeper than the services. If you're a dentist, please don't tell me that you offer supreme care for teeth. I hope that's a given. No one wants to go to an average dentist, nor would you advertise that your teeth cleaning services are pretty average. Tell me about the experience. Appeal to my senses as a consumer—what will it feel like, taste like, smell like, sound like—as many of those points as you can touch on. Pull at my heart strings here.

"But Trib, you can't smell a medical practice!" Oh yeah? What if you're an ENT? You can inspire a feeling around being able to smell. I cannot stress enough how important it is to talk about how people will feel when they do business with you. You have to inspire a feeling, and perform those actions that will enhance that feeling. People want to

www.thehealthcareplaybook.com

know how doing business with you will feel, and what they could potentially miss out on by NOT doing business with you. This is called creating FOMO, or Fear Of Missing Out.

This is how FOMO works: "Order while supplies last."

"We're giving away free tee shirts to the first 200 subscribers."

"Buy one now and we will throw in an additional one for free; but hurry, this offer is only good for the next 10 minutes."

"Wouldn't it feel great to be the first person in your neighborhood with this new home feature?"

"Creating 'wow,' one backyard barbecue at a time."

All of these statements are widely used in advertising and marketing. There's no doubt that all of you reading this have heard or experienced these in one way or another. I want you to think about how these statements inspire a feeling inside of you. Who doesn't love getting free shit, like a tee shirt? Who doesn't love a BOGO deal? Who wouldn't want to feel good about how their backyard appeals to their guests. All of these statements are designed to make you feel like you could miss out on something, and to motivate you to take action now. Not later. Not when convenience strikes you, but NOW. While these are not mission statements, they are good examples of the feelings you want to inspire with your mission statement.

Now you're wondering, "Well, how do I do that?"

But even more so, you're probably thinking, "These are all products. How does this apply to medical practices?" Fear not, I'm going to show you.

Unf*cking Private Healthcare

The mission statement at my regenerative medicine practice is this: Our mission is to give you a better way of healing. Return you to work, play, and life with confidence and joy. Get you off addictive pain medicines. Eliminate reoccurring doctor visits. And even better, you will rediscover the joy of life and feel younger again.

Do you see how this statement inspires feeling? We're talking about the opportunity to feel youthful again. And that feeling of youth is specific to the person that is reading that statement. Youthful doesn't necessarily mean we're knocking 20 years off the clock. We're giving you the opportunity to feel like your more youthful self—whatever that means for you as one of our patients.

Maybe you haven't been able to play golf for 5 years because of shoulder pain, and you miss the hell out of it. Everyone keeps saying that you need to have surgery to fix it, but you don't want to because surgery is a long recovery process, and there's no guarantee that you would be able to play golf again anyway. So you just limit your activity and take a handful of medicines to manage the pain on a regular basis, until the pain becomes too much and you say, "The hell with it. Let's do the surgery."

If I can inspire you to feel that our services can give you your life back and (here's the big part) actually deliver on that promise, how big of a fan would you become of our services? This statement also motivates the person I'm talking to, to take action so that they can have that feeling of youth returned; so they can get back on the golf course, and so they can stop with the overuse of medicines to manage their life. Imagine for a second that you have been suffering with back pain for years. You've had surgery. You still have pain and have to take medicine to manage it. You haven't been able to work, play with your kids, or enjoy your favorite past time on a Sunday afternoon with your buddies—and you come across this mission statement. Even if you're jaded by what you have been through, and healthcare has left a bad taste in your mouth, this statement is something that at the very least

36

www.thehealthcareplaybook.com

will peak your interest and move you to find out more. Which leads us into discussing how to properly use these statements.

I want you to think for a moment about how you introduce yourself. Let's say you are at a cocktail party, and somebody comes up to you and says, "Hi, I'm John Smith," as he sticks his hand out to shake yours.

You respond, "Nice to meet you. I'm Pocahontas."

"What do you do, Pocahontas?"

"I'm a doctor."

"Oh, really? What kind?"

"I'm in regenerative medicine."

This is typically how the conversation goes, right? Nothing meaningful happens. You're just going through the polite progression of conversation without even exchanging anything of value. John Smith hasn't in any way, shape, form, or fashion been sparked to want to continue a deeper conversation with Pocahontas. In fact, because the human brain is programmed to do two things, thrive and survive, John Smith is probably more concerned with the bacon wrapped dates that just passed behind him, and the fact that his cocktail is running low, than he is about the fact that Pocahontas is a doctor.

Let's look at how you can use your vision and mission statement to invoke a deeper conversation.

"Hi. I'm John Smith."

"Nice to meet you. I'm Pocahontas."

"What do you do, Pocahontas?"

"I'm in the business of stopping the overuse of medications and unwarranted surgery." (powerful vision and why statement)

The next question will inevitably be, "How do you do that, Pocahontas?"

"By offering people a better way of healing through stem cell therapy and regenerative medicine. People deserve to be working, playing, and enjoying life. I help people rediscover their youth." (mission and value)

"Are you a doctor, Pocahontas?"

"Yes, I am. I specialize in the spine and joints."

This exchange will, without a doubt, draw John Smith in to a deeper conversation, because Pocahontas led with WHY she does what she does. "Why" will always lead to "how" and "what," and ultimately to an open-ended conversation. Remember, people don't care what you do. They care how what you do is going to help them. So, tell them exactly how what you do will help them get back to the sport they love, deliver a baby with ease, have perfect skin, make sure their child is safe, etc.

Your vision statement should be on your business card, all over your website, and all over your social media, and it should be plastered on the wall in a couple of different places in your office, in a place where your patients can see it as well as your team. Your mission statement is typically longer, so it won't go on your business card, but it should be present digitally and be posted in your office. We will talk more about digital and hard marketing in the coming chapters, and how you can effectively use both your vision and mission statements on these platforms.

www.thehealthcareplaybook.com

Here's your action step! Go to www.thehealthcareplaybook.com/ booktools, and print the mission and vision statement worksheet. This will help you identify those key components you need in order to create these statements.

Now, let's get into how you can use your mission and vision statements with your team. After all, if they aren't on board, and they aren't feeling it, neither will your patients.

Chapter 4

Rallying Your Team Behind Your Leadership

At this point, we have identified the WHY behind your brand. We've walked your potential patients through a tangible journey of what doing business with you looks and feels like. We've identified proper vision and mission statements and how to write them. Now it's time to put these pieces to work for you—right? Yes! And no.

We have to address your team first, and make sure you have the right people in place that will exude your why, your mission, and your vision. The definition of the word "team," as a noun, according to Merriam-Webster, is: "A number of persons associated together in work or activity." While this definition is pretty general, the word "team," defined as a verb, states this: "To put together in a coordinated ensemble. To join forces or efforts." In other words, a team is a group of individuals who join forces or efforts in a coordinated ensemble to achieve a common goal. Think about that for a second. Are the people who work with you coordinated and aligned around a common goal? Do they understand what they are actually there for, and for what specific reason? And even more so, is it just a job for them?

The way you put together your team is often done wrong from the get go. The problems start when interviewing and hiring. Most healthcare professionals and healthcare offices hire based upon experience or based upon a resume. You look for people who have experience in healthcare offices, experience as a medical assistant, experience as a medical secretary, experience in submitting claims, or experience in answering phones and scheduling patients. Notice a pattern here? Every hiring decision is based upon experience. This is a huge problem, and not because experience isn't important, but because most of you have not grasped the idea that skills can be taught, and personalities cannot. In other words, you should be hiring based upon personality rather than on experience.

I mentioned earlier in the book that nobody cares how good you are at your profession if you are an asshole. The same could be said about the team you're hiring. Just because they have experience and they're good at what they do, doesn't mean they will be right for your practice. Their experience has zero to do with how much they believe in your vision. Their experience has zero to do with how well they will treat your patients. Their experience only tells me one thing: that they may possess the skills necessary to do a job.

Don't you think it would also be necessary to know things such as if they work well with a team or if they are lone wolves? What are their personal goals for their professional future? How are they best motivated? How do they approach problem solving? Are they proactive or reactive? Do they have "toward" or "away from" habits? Are they motivated by opportunities to do things a different way, or do they prefer to follow a step-by-step process? What factors influence their decision making? How do they work in a stressful environment?

Seems like a lot to consider, right? The problem is, if you don't consider the answers to these questions, you could be hiring a team of completely different people, who operate and interpret information in completely different ways, which sets your practice up for communication issues. Don't get me wrong; you definitely want to have a team with different strengths so that it's well rounded. However, you want to make sure that certain personality traits fit the style of office and the position you are hiring for. Let me explain.

www.thehealthcareplaybook.com

Let's start with proactive versus reactive. A proactive person is someone who initiates and jumps right in without analyzing the depth of the problem at hand. They will get the job done and, at the extreme, give little to no consideration for other people. If you have a marketing or sales person on your staff, this is probably them. You would want them to be. A reactive person will wait for others to initiate while they analyze and respond to requests. This a role better suited for your medical assistant or medical secretary. If you had a very proactive medical assistant/secretary, it could set you up for some conflict, as most healthcare professionals have pretty large egos. Don't deny it; you know it's true. And if you're thinking that the ego thing isn't true, you're most likely the person that I'm speaking to.

In Shelle Rose Charvet's book, *Words That Change Minds,* she discusses the concept of moving away from or moving toward something. Are you moving toward goals or away from problems, she asks. "Toward" types of people are motivated to achieve goals, and "away from" types of people are motivated to solve or avoid problems. I will go ahead and tell you that most consumers approach healthcare with a very "away from" type of outlook. People look to get out of pain or get over being sick. Most healthcare consumers don't even consider going to a doctor until there is a problem. This a proactive, "away from" type of situation. These people are actively trying to move away from a problem. So, to best solve this problem, you may want to consider that the person you are hiring to take calls and do your scheduling be just as proactive, but focused on the "toward" goals. This will match the proactive energy of most of the people calling your office and wanting to get well, and will also be the solution to their desire of getting better. The consumer wants to move away from illness, and you have the solution to move them toward that goal. These are also good traits to have as a sales person. Hint: The person that answers your phone and greets your patients should have a sales type of mindset. This person is the most important person to your practice. Sorry to crush your ego some more here, but patients

Unf*cking Private Healthcare

never see you, the practitioner, if the "gatekeeper" can't get them on your schedule. More on this idea later.

Let's go over one more of these personality traits that I think is important, because it relates to your office manager or practice administrator. The most important thing you want to consider for this person is their ability to get shit done. You're probably thinking, "What does that have to do with personality?" Again, I won't disappoint you; I'll tell you. If your practice administrator is a wildly creative person who likes to innovate, they will most likely come up with really great ideas on how to maximize patient care, better billing procedures, better tactics for the team to rally around, etc. These are your WHY people. But they potentially won't be really good at developing strategies and implementing these changes. If they are more of a procedures type, or a HOW type of person, they will be more inclined to follow a plan or a tried and true set of procedures. These are your implementers. The problem with these folks is that they won't have new innovative ways to solve new problems. They will be stumped at what to do if there isn't a procedure in place. So, you have to decide what type of person you want at the helm. In my experience, when you have a creative person calling the plays, and the rest of the team are procedures people who can execute the plan, shit gets done, and it gets done in a magical way. You need to match your creative people with your procedure people. This is the beginning of team development.

How do you figure out who is who? It's quite simple. Ask if they prefer to follow a plan that has already been set up, or if they prefer to have their own plan. When asking about proactive and reactive, inquire about how they prefer to solve problems. Do they jump right in and troubleshoot on the spot, or do they prefer to analyze first? Finding out the "toward" or the "away" portion is a little more tricky, because it requires you to listen to their responses. For example, I may ask a candidate if they prefer to problem solve by jumping right in or by analyzing. Let's say they give the answer, "Jump right in." I'll

www.thehealthcareplaybook.com

immediately ask why they feel that is important. Their answer will lead me to know whether they are jumping right in because they want to solve a problem (away from), or because the issue is keeping them from getting shit done (toward).

I have included a print-ready version of some interview questions and how to interpret the answers based on the type of personality you are looking to hire. You can find it and print it at www.thehealthcareplay book.com/booktools.

Using these tools to help you put together the right team is your first step in being a good leader. The next step is going to be discovering what each person on your team desires for their professional growth. Believe it or not, most people have a desire or a vision for themselves as a professional, and I hate to tell you this, but it's probably not working for $14/hour at your practice answering phones. Good leaders will show up powerfully to help their teams grow. As your team grows, guess what else happens to your practice? It grows. Tada!!

I go back to the conversation between the CEO and CFO. The CEO is concerned with the growth of the company, and the CFO with how money is spent within the company.

CEO: "We need to put some training in place to help advance our people."

CFO: "Training is expensive."

CEO: "I realize that, but if we don't develop our team, we will never be able to grow this company."

CFO: "What if we spend all this money on training and developing our employees, and they decide to leave to go work somewhere else?"

Unf*cking Private Healthcare

CEO: "What if we don't and they stay?"

You must realize that when you build people up professionally, you are inviting growth into your business, and into your life and theirs. Find out what each one of your staff members wants for their future, and help them get it! This is another step in becoming a better leader.

John Mattone, author of The Intelligent Leader, talks about having a duty mindset. You have a duty to your team, not just your patients. Many healthcare practice owners always think about their patients and getting their patients taken care of, but neglect to put their team first. When you put your team first, they will put your patients first. Read that again.

Have lunch with each one of them, and learn their desires for their futures. Ask them about your practice. Ask them what they love about it, and ask what things they would like to see change. Ask them how they view you as a leader. Uh oh, did you just shit your pants thinking about what they would say? If you did, good! In order to be a better leader, you have to find out where you excel and where you may have gaps. You should also be able to drop the ego and be vulnerable enough to listen to what they have to say in regards to your leadership, without getting offended or mad. Being vulnerable is the key word here. Gone are the hard nose days of rough, tough, don't take no shit off anybody type of leadership mentalities. You cannot effectively lead your team if you are not aware of who you are and how you lead. Show some gratitude that your team was honest enough to share with you how they feel about your practice and your leadership. Set a safe place where they can be open and honest and not feel they will be reprimanded. Then take action on those things they share with you, because what good is gathering information if you don't act upon it?

Here's the thing, though. Most of you will go to work right away on the things you fall short on. You concentrate on the things that your team told you was lacking in your leadership and/or practice. This is a

www.thehealthcareplaybook.com

mistake. Start by building upon the things that you already do well, while being aware of the things that you don't do well. Self-educate on how you can start getting better at those gaps. Be vulnerable enough to allow your staff to remind you when those shortcomings arise, so that you can continue to make necessary changes in that regard. No one will ever be perfect as a leader. It's the pursuit of perfection that will set you apart.

If you have never taken a class on core values, I highly recommend it. Core values are a necessary part of understanding how you lead. Your inner core, which are your values, beliefs, and character, is what will inspire your team. These are the reasons you are who you are. These are the things that your employees will want to show off about where they work and the services you provide. Your outer core are your competencies and performance, and are usually the things you get graded on in a yearly review if you're an employee. News flash: No one cares what you do, or how good you are at what you do, if you're an asshole. I've said this multiple times. This is what separates inner core values and outer core values. Just because you have a strong work ethic, doesn't mean people want to work for you or with you. It's the inner core values that show up in your leadership that make people want to work with you and show off your practice. Yes, your team should want to show off where they work, to anyone and everyone that could benefit from the services you provide. I'm hoping I don't need to tell you which of those 2 values, inner core or outer core, you need to concentrate on the most to make that happen. You don't get to be the star of the show without the supporting cast. Remember that.

As you begin to establish new relationships with your team, and invite positivity into your practice, your culture will begin to change for the positive. Culture is like the glue that holds everything together within your practice. It's the framework from which people find motivation and a desire to work for and with you. And it will inspire people to act upon your vision and mission.

Unf*cking Private Healthcare

Remember the part of my regenerative medicine practice vision statement that read, "...You will rediscover the joy of life...?" Do you think any of our patients will experience joy if they don't feel joy coming from our team when they walk in the door? How do you create joy in your team? Simple; do all the things I am suggesting in this book! Put together the right team that will align with the right vision and mission, and be a good steward and leader for your team. This will no doubt create a strong culture that every person who does business with you will feel! Remember, the key word is "feel."

Remember when I said that most healthcare practitioners are a skill away from being truly great? Ask yourself if leadership is that skill you need. If so, take action on improving that part of yourself while continuing to build upon the things you are already good at. A good leader recognizes where they are great and where they need to improve. Keeping your staff involved in your personal growth will allow them to feel part of something greater, rather than just an employee.

Spend time with your staff on a regular basis. Schedule team meetings that have objectives and goals. Spend time talking about what works well and what needs to improve. Spend time educating your team in areas where they want to learn more. Give them the floor to openly voice concerns and ideas of how to improve certain systems within the practice, without feeling that they will be reprimanded for speaking up. And if there is to be some reprimand for a just reason, be sure it happens behind closed doors. The rule is always to coach in public and reprimand behind closed doors.

The overall health of your team and their ability to rally around a common goal and mission will forever change the culture of your practice. This change in culture will ultimately change the response from your patients. It is your responsibility as the owner and a physician to control the culture of your practice. Once you do this, you can then rally your team around your mission.

www.thehealthcareplaybook.com

If your vision is to do great things and see massive changes in the world, and you have put a strategic mission in place that builds you toward that vision, you can then engage your team in following through on those steps. For example, in my practice's mission statement, there is a portion that states, "Return you to work, play, and life..." The reason that there are choices here is because you need to identify what is important to your patient. Why are they in your office? What are they hoping to gain? How do you get that information? Yet again, it's simple. Think about it like this: A real estate agent that takes two hours to show you an entire house, or an entire day to show you multiple houses, without actually asking you what the most important part of the house is, won't satisfy what's important to you. On the other hand, a real estate agent that asks what's important to you first, may find out that the kitchen is the most important part to you. Now, that agent has a game plan! You must find out what is most important to your patients. Ask them, "Hey, what's the most important thing for you to get out of your visit here today?" Or, "What's the most important thing for you when you come to any doctor's office?" This type of questioning shows that you're actually interested in what your patient is interested in. Don't assume everyone is there just to "feel better." Find out WHY they want to feel better. What will they be able to do when they feel better? What is really at the core of their desire to clear up their skin, get over their back pain, be a mother for the 5th time, etc.?

There is a reason I put that particular clause in my mission statement for my regenerative medicine practice. It shows that I give a damn about what people want to get back to. I care about why they are in my office, and so does my team. Imagine if your patients walk into your office and, from the time they set foot in the door until the time they step out of it, they are constantly having what's important to them actually handed to them. And handed to them by every single person in the office. This is rallying your team around a mission. This is changing the culture of your practice. This is feeding your vision. This is the beginning step of customer service and creating raving fans,

Unf*cking Private Healthcare

which is what we will be talking about in the next chapter. Creating the opportunity to make someone feel good, will always make you look good.

Let's go create some raving fans!

Chapter 5

Sales and Customer Service: One and the Same

There is an old saying, "People don't care how much you know until they know how much you care." Showing someone how much you care is compassion and customer service. Sales, when done correctly, is also about showing people you care. This chapter will probably be a defining moment for you in realizing that you are, in fact, in sales. You and every person on your team and on your staff is in sales. Sales is customer service, and customer service is sales. Sales is about people. Customer service is about people. They are one and the same. Everything is sales. You are either selling—your services, your products, your ideas, your goods—or being sold to by someone who is trying to sell you their goods, ideas, products, or services. Sales and customer service will either be your biggest asset or your biggest liability. As we move through this chapter, I will continuously tie customer service and sales together; and by the end, hopefully, you will realize that you are not in the medical business but in the people business, and people deserve good customer service.

A lot of you are thinking, "I'm not a salesman. I'm not a sales person. I hate sales people." I get it. You aren't wrong. There are a few of those shady-ass crooked people who have ruined the word "sales," and given it a negative connotation. When someone says "sales," your immediate reaction is probably, "Ugh." You picture that sales-y used car dealership guy with the creeper mustache. I get it. But guess what? There are some healthcare providers that have done the same thing to the medical field. It doesn't necessarily mean that you're one of

Unf*cking Private Healthcare

them. I'm going to show you how to sell people on why you do what you do, and then get them to buy what you do, while giving them a great experience. That is sales. It's what Ken Blanchard refers to as "delivery +1," in his book, Creating Raving Fans. This is a chapter for your entire team to get behind, especially if you have ancillary products and services in your practice that are cash pay services.

Remember when we discussed the fact that most consumers have very low expectations of healthcare offices? Refer back to the chart I had you create in Chapter 2. One of the columns in that chart is called the "value" section. This is what you are giving your patients that will keep them coming back and telling more and more people about you. This chapter is how you deliver on those values. These are the reasons people will pass other practices while driving to yours. It's the same reason you might choose one movie theater over another, even though the one you like is further from your home. Every movie theater is pretty much showing the same movies at any given time, but one might have more comfortable seats, or serve you a real meal, or has an easier way to book online, or the staff may be friendlier and more personable. It's the reason you choose one particular gas station on a corner where 3 other ones exist. Maybe the particular gas station you like fills up the car for you, always calls you by name, always cleans your windshield, always hands you a bottle of water, and generates conversation with you. At this point, you are no longer concerned about cost. It has nothing to do with price. It has to do with being sold on the service. And maybe you pay a little more for this service, but guess what? You don't give a damn, because the value is so much better. And yes, there are still areas in the United States where gas is not self-service.

Places like the movie theatre and the gas station I mentioned above have committed to a certain level of service. They are committed to their WHY, and they have decided to deliver on that each and every day. They are sold on their models and do everything necessary to maintain good service. Are you sold on the service you provide to your

www.thehealthcareplaybook.com

patients? If you were a consumer, would you come to your office? Would your staff choose your office as the place they would go to for all their needs as it relates to their bodily pains, skin care, GI issues, or chiropractic needs? How can your staff adequately describe what it's like to do business at your office if your staff has never used the products or services in your office? It's time to find out who on your team is sold on what you do. Are they sold on the processes, services, and products you deliver? If not, you better find out why. Ask yourself if you would buy a product from a sales person who has never used the product they are selling.

"Oh, this is the best skin care line on the market. You just gotta have it."

"Do you use it?"

"Well, no."

"Then how do you know it's the best?"

How could you claim or announce to someone that your products or services are the best if you or your team have never used them? Gut-check moment again for you as a practice owner or physician. Now is the time to get sold on the service and products you deliver. If you and your team are not sold on the service you provide, you better believe it is time to change that. The other OB/GYN office down the street that is killing it, most likely has already done this. Now is the time to get your staff involved in those products and services as well. How the hell could I run a regenerative medicine practice, and talk about the benefits, if I had never had a procedure done with my own services. The answer is, I couldn't. The answer is also yes; I have had a regenerative medicine procedure done. And the results were amazing! People on my staff have utilized our services as well. They wouldn't be able to SELL any of our patients on the benefits of what we do if they themselves had never experienced it. If you and your team are

Unf*cking Private Healthcare

not sold on the service and products you offer, they won't be able to advocate for you or tell potential patients why they should come to your office to be treated. That's serving the customer. That's selling your team on why you do what you do. Do you see how sales and customer service begins to come together?

For those of you who love the "ethical" side of this coin, let me open your mind up to what is unethical when it comes to sales. It is unethical to preach about your services or products when you have never used them. It is unethical to not offer supreme customer service. It is unethical to not sell someone a product or service that could help them achieve a goal, no matter what that goal is. How people are treated should always come first. This is sales. This is customer service.

Let's further the discussion by looking at some practical things around your office. The terms "check-in desk" and "check-out desk" are 2 of the most ridiculous names for those 2 areas in your office. You are actively planting a seed in the minds of your patients that closes off any sort of deeper relationship. Checking out plants the idea that business has concluded, and anything from this point on is stopping me from getting out of your office. You close in your check-in area by putting sliding glass doors in front of it. Nothing screams compassion, service, and welcome more than sliding glass closing me off from communication. Think about this. What if it was called a welcome desk? What if there was no sliding glass, and the person that greeted you was actually welcoming and obliged to meet you. They aren't staring at you over a computer, with the phone pinched between their shoulder and ear. They thank you for your time and genuinely inquire about how you are doing. They offer you a bottle of water or a coffee, and hand you a napkin. If it's your first visit at their practice, they might ask you, "What's the most important thing for you when you come to a healthcare office?"

www.thehealthcareplaybook.com

"Hi, good morning. Thank you for taking the time to come in to see Dr. Brown, and for choosing our office for your care today. I'm Samantha," she says, with hand outstretched.

"Hi Samantha. I'm Jimmy Jones. I have an appointment with Dr. Brown today at 10."

"Perfect. This is your first time here, correct?"

"It is."

"Wonderful. Tell me, Mr. Jones, what's the most important thing for you when you come to a doctor's office? Timeliness in getting you out? Time with the doctor to have your questions answered? How can I make your visit satisfactory for you?"

"I usually do have to cancel half my work day any time I make a doctor's appointment, because I'm never sure how long I'm going to have to wait."

"I agree that must be frustrating. I will make a note on your chart so that our nurses, assistants, and doctor all know that time is important to you. We will do our very best to make sure we get you in and out without rushing through your appointment."

"That would be amazing. Thank you."

"You're welcome. Here's a bottle of water and a napkin. If you'll have a seat, I'll bring the iPad around to you and show you quickly how to fill out the necessary paperwork. It seems no matter how hard we try to eliminate it, there's always more paperwork."

If you think for one second that this isn't selling, you're absolutely crazy. Samantha is sold on the fact that she needs to cater to what's important to Mr. Jones. Mr. Jones most likely has never been greeted

Unf*cking Private Healthcare

in this fashion at any healthcare office, and if the office follows through on providing him great care for the reason he came in, and great service, he will undoubtedly be sold on his experience. He will tell everyone about it. This is delivery +1.

I can hear you now. "We don't have time to do all that shit. I'd have to hire 2 more people just to do that. My front office staff has to call this insurance company and handle this phone call, and it costs too much to hire more..." excuses, excuses, excuses. Cut the shit. As a consumer, you would value this type of service no matter where you were, right? Grocery store, movies, restaurant—it wouldn't matter. And if a place gave you bad service, you wouldn't go back. You wouldn't advertise to anyone how much you loved that store or restaurant, right? The extraordinary service you got, sold you on that place and made you want to go back again and tell all your friends to go too. So why wouldn't you have a burning desire to provide the same service at your practice? You can't afford it? You can't afford NOT to do it.

Let's go back to Samantha for a second, because I want to make sure you understand how important her role is in making your office the difference between 2 stars and 5 stars. Samantha's role in all this is to be your sales person—the sales person for your values and what you stand for as a business owner. If she sucks at delivering that, then the overall impression of your practice is that it sucks too. This can all be determined in the mind of the consumer before they even see you, the actual doctor, physician, therapist, etc. Samantha becomes the face of your company way before you do. Samantha's role is to sell you, your office, and your practice, way before your patients even step in the door. Her role is the most important role in your office. Whoever it is that answers the phone and greets people when they first walk in the door is setting the tone for the type of service your patients receive. Think about that. Is the right person answering the phone in your office? Are they conveying the right message about what your office stands for? Are they completely sold on what you do as a

www.thehealthcareplaybook.com

provider, and completely sold on the services you offer? Or are they just punching a time clock and putting on a smile as best they can?

When your team is completely sold on the values of your mission, vision, and on you as a leader, they will be delighted to work in your office. They will become raving fans before your patients do. This is essential. If your team isn't a fan of your practice or your values, how will they ever make your patients feel valued? What if you have ancillaries that are cash pay? Does your team know about those products or services and why they are beneficial?

If you have ancillary services in your practice, you must have sales people on your team that are skilled in selling these products or services. Most offices put these items in a glass case, or flood the lobby with brochures and rack cards to advertise those products, but they do nothing to determine if those products are desirable by their patient base. Then you further compound the situation by offering dozens of expired magazines, and trash TV, which distracts from those ancillary services. We will talk more about your lobby in the next chapters, and how you should set it up to further sell your services or products. In the case of ancillary services and products, why not have a health questionnaire or checklist as a part of your initial patient documentation? You could simply ask people what other services they would be interested in, and provide them a list of those services. Have them pick three. This gets passed on to the medical assistant and the doctor, and becomes part of the appointment. Many of you think that if you just put a sign up that says, "We offer Botox," people will automatically think to themselves, "Wow. I can get Botox done here too." While that does happen occasionally, a piece of paper you printed and stuck with scotch tape to a door in your lobby, will only work marginally at best.

Why are checklists or health questionnaires necessary for selling those services? Because if helps define what people want. Selling is about

Unf*cking Private Healthcare

filling a need or a desire. You can only fulfill that need or desire if you find out that person's needs, wants, or problems. If you just start rattling off these services and their benefits randomly, you will lose the sale because you haven't identified what people actually want. But if you can identify their interests and wants, and it is in their face from the time they walk in; and they show interest on the paperwork they fill out, and it's mentioned by the staff and the doctor at the conclusion of the appointment, guess what happens? It's this magical thing called selling it. Selling happens when you actively find out what satisfies a need or want, and you deliver it!

Think about it like this: If I go to buy a new car, and the first sales person I talk to starts rattling off all the technical garbage about the car—"It goes zero to 60 in 2.5 seconds. It has a 7.2 L, V10 engine that's twin turbo supercharged, and LED lights that blink on the dash to indicate you're in prime driving mode. It's got this suspension system that allows you take a turn at 9,000 mph. It's got...."—seriously, you lost me. Some of you might be into that kind of thing. Good for you. I'm not. I want to know my child will be safe in the car. I travel a lot, so I want to know about the gas mileage. I want to know how the service plan on the vehicle works, and if it's going to cost me an arm and a leg. I care about totally different things than what this idiot is rattling off. It would be different if he had started the conversation by saying, "Hi. Thanks for your time today. Glad you came to our dealership. Tell me, what are the 3 most important things to you when you're buying a car?" Now he knows where to start and what to show me. He may even further this discovery by asking what my budget is, so that he can really narrow it down. And if he's really good, he will show me cars over my budget. Tip: Don't ever start with the budget question. People don't buy solely based upon price, and price is usually never the real objection when it comes to making a purchase. The real objection is typically the perceived value for the price. If someone has an objection to the price of the services you offer, it's usually because you haven't built the value up enough to justify the cost. Don't sell people based on price. Sell people based on the value of satisfying a need. And

www.thehealthcareplaybook.com

never, ever lower your price when people object to it. Defend your prices by building the value of the service or product. Always defend the price; never discount the price.

I mentioned the word "discovery" a paragraph and a half ago. This word was used on purpose. Anytime someone calls your office to inquire about services, this is what I mean by discovery. Discovery is not, "What insurance plan do you have?" Or, "What's the reason for the visit?" These potential patients expect to be asked these boring-ass, non-invitational questions from any and every healthcare office they call. Please be better than this. Train your team on how to actually gather information, and find out what is important to your potential patients. There is a process that Denise, our practice administrator, uses when she trains our team on how to do this. Denise is an absolute ninja at converting leads into paying appointments. The reason she is so good at converting? She gives a damn about the person more than getting the appointment. Once you show you care about the person on the other end of the phone, the appointment gets made naturally.

A discovery call is about collecting information from patients about their desires. It's about making that initial connection and building rapport, and oozing your values by showing true interest in what that person is going through, and what they are looking to achieve by coming to your practice. It's pulling out their "why" as it relates to needing an appointment. There is always an underlying reason, other than "feeling better," that people desire. It's not just getting over knee pain. It could be getting over knee pain so that they can run again. It could be that they are looking for a new OB/GYN office because they had a previous tough pregnancy and are concerned about going through that again. You never know why people call unless you ask them. Once you have built up the relationship enough to get this information, you can then talk to them about how you can help them solve the problem. The problem is not the back pain. It's the fact they can't get up and down off the floor to play with their grandchild. Speak to them about that issue and how your services can remedy that, and

Unf*cking Private Healthcare

you'll get the appointment. But even more so, you will have already laid a foundation of trust and value. This is sales. This is customer service.

In conclusion, always remember: You're not selling skin care; you're selling glowing skin that attracts compliments. You're not selling regenerative medicine or stem cell therapy; you're selling hope to people in pain. You're not selling OB/GYN services; you're offering care that women can relate to. You're not selling clean teeth at your dentist office; you're selling a bright, cheerful smile. Always, always, always, sell to a feeling that matches a desire; not a budget. Always deliver +1. Going the extra mile will always create raving fans for your practice, which in turn creates the most valuable resource for returning clients and referrals. After all, the person that already knows, likes, and trusts you will always be the best source of further sales for your practice.

If you and your team need help polishing your sales and customer service skills, go to www.tripointmed.com, and schedule a 60-minute call with me—yes, it will actually be me. We can discuss your practice, your team, and what your values are, and put a plan in place on how to create raving fans.

In the next couple of chapters, we will begin to look at this thing called marketing. We are going to dive into hard marketing and digital marketing strategies that you can begin using immediately, which will help draw attention to your services. Many of you are doing this wrong, and I'm going to call you out on it. Get ready to change your marketing, using the new message and new customer service experience you've learned so far.

Chapter 6

Intro to Marketing – Hard Marketing

Marketing: What comes to your mind when you think about that word? What is marketing? How do you market properly? How do you get the right message out there in the hands of all the right people? How do you stand out?

Well, the good news is that you've (hopefully) used the tools I've given you so far to identify how to differentiate your practice from all the others. Now we have to talk about how to get people interested enough to come and see you. Let's first start by properly defining what marketing is not, and what shitty marketing looks like.

Marketing is NOT your message. Marketing is NOT limited to lead generation. Those companies that tell you that they can generate an extra 30 leads a month that we're inundated with, don't offer the full spectrum of what it means to capture people and draw them in. After all, what good is 30 leads a month if you can't close them—this goes back to our chapter on customer service and sales. Marketing is not all the pretty pictures and insider language you use to justify your practice and intelligence. And contrary to common belief, you don't have to have a million-dollar monthly marketing budget to get noticed. Does it help? Of course, but it's not necessary.

According to Merriam-Webster, marketing is defined as "the process or technique of promoting, selling, and distributing a product or service." Put simply, it's how you tell people about what you do or

61

Unf*cking Private Healthcare

offer that gets them to take action. It's the delivery of the message you have put together in your branding. Marketing is not branding, and branding is not marketing. Marketing is the delivery of your brand into the market place that hopefully inspires people to do business with you, or to desire an outcome that only you can provide for them. You must be omnipresent in the delivery of your message, getting your message out there on every available platform, where people can see it, hear it, touch it, smell it, etc. Yes, every platform—social media, TV, email, snail mail, podcast interviews, local business groups such as a chamber of commerce, your signage, your website, your business card, magazines, newspapers—everywhere. Twenty-five years ago, it used to take 7–10 touch points to get people to remember your brand, product, or service. Today, with the amount of media that is thrown at us, that number is closer to 27–30. There are constant distractions out there, and nearly 3000 commercials that our brains are experiencing every day, so if you want to stand out and get noticed, you have to be EVERYWHERE—omnipresent.

There is a common acronym used in marketing and advertising called AIDA. It stands for Attention, Interest, Desire, and Action. This is not just some cheesy acronym that marketers made up along the way. It was actually coined in the late 1800s by E. St. Elmo Lewis. It is an illustration of how consumers move through cognitive and affective thinking stages, and eventually end up at a behavioral stage. As consumers, we move through a hierarchy of effects that cannot be ignored. It's similar to learning to play an instrument. You will not be able to pick up a guitar and play a Jimmy Hendrix song without first understanding the strings and where to put your fingers. Just like it takes practice to learn how to play a guitar, you must take your potential patients on a journey through these steps, in order to get them to do business with you. These steps include a cognitive processing stage, or a learning stage, where they become aware of your service and want to know more about it; then an affective processing stage, where feelings or interest will eventually move the consumer to taking action. It looks something like this:

www.thehealthcareplaybook.com

Attention: A potential consumer becomes aware of your service.

Interest: That consumer then becomes interested in what you offer.

Desire: They will feel or desire the outcome or service you provide.

Action: They take action by scheduling or calling to inquire.

You must move your potential patients through this funnel in order to get their attention, peak their interest, inspire a feeling to want what you have to offer, and ultimately move them to do business with you. This is purely a stimulus-response model.

There is one other area that a lot of people, including myself, feel should be added to this acronym. That would be the "R" or Retention area. What steps are you taking to ensure your patients continue to come and see you, or be a source of other new patients? How do you retain their loyalty? This last section I feel is definitely one that a lot of healthcare offices don't focus on. You are constantly wanting to draw new people in, but you aren't focused on driving business and demand within a community that already knows, likes, and trusts you. Nor are you concerned with keeping contact with them on a regular basis other than when they "need" your services or when it's time for their yearly follow-up.

I also want to introduce to you this idea of empathy and authority. Too often, I see healthcare providers talk about themselves: how up to date their facility is; how great their team is; how they are the number 1 cardiologist in all the land, and graduated magna cum laude from Harvard med school. Shoot me. Again, no one cares what you know until they know how much you care. The rule is that you don't get to talk about yourself until you have talked about the needs of your patients. Empathy is defined as "the ability to understand the feelings of another." This is how it works:

Unf*cking Private Healthcare

"At Dr. Brown's office, we understand what it's like to be sick and not able to move through your day with energy and joy. That's why we're committed to providing you the most personable care and expertise in your time of need. Our doctors are highly skilled and trained in delivering you the best medicine for your specific needs."

Empathy. Then authority.

In this chapter, we're going to look at hard marketing strategies and how to apply the concepts I mentioned above. By hard marketing, I am referring to tangible items like mailers, signage, rack cards, brochures, etc. In the next chapter, we will look at the digital forms of marketing. For those of you that are wondering about social media and websites, that chapter is where we will discuss those things.

Before we get started on the actual items themselves, let's talk about a few pain points and potential distractions your patients experience, which you should be aware of when it comes to marketing. These are things that are confusing and distracting people from doing business with you. Let's start with your lobby. One strategic place where your marketing materials should exist, which the majority of you neglect to set up properly, is your lobby. This area is where your patients will spend the majority of their time. It should be advertising and selling for you!

I can't tell you how stupid it is for your lobby to be cluttered with piles of expired magazines, and to have trash TV on your screens. I am often amazed at how many healthcare offices do this. When you go to a restaurant, do they offer you a menu from a competing restaurant? When you go to buy a new car from a particular dealership, do they advertise cars of a different brand? NO! They only provide you with materials that talk about their products or services. So, why do a lot of healthcare practices flood their lobbies with distractions? Your lobby should be advertising and advocating for what it is you have to offer. Take the magazines out. The TV is better OFF than showing CNN

www.thehealthcareplaybook.com

or HGTV. Use your lobby to show people what you offer. Put flyers, brochures, and rack cards of the services you offer, on all the tables. Put up awards you have won. Place pull up banners in the corners, and pamphlets that talk about the ancillary services you provide. Make available only the services and products you offer. Put QR codes in plastic holders that allow people to scan them to get more information on your social media sites. Invite them to follow you or leave a review for you, using these QR codes. (If you don't know what a QR code is, we will touch more on their significance when we discuss digital marketing.) You could even put a book of written testimonials on the table for people to look at. Whatever you put in your lobby, make sure it markets for you and not for anything else. Most importantly, make sure the language you use is something people actually understand.

This brings me to my next pet peeve: insider language. Most of you are killing me with the medical talk. As a healthcare provider, I know what lateral epicondylitis is. I understand lumbar radiculopathy, ectopic pregnancy, eczema, and encephalitis. Everyday people don't! Stop using those terms in your materials. Tell people about back pain, elbow pain, swelling in the brain, and red, swollen, itchy skin. And more importantly, how you understand the feelings they have around those conditions. What solution do you have to offer them? Did you know that the majority of people in the world relate to language on a 5th grade level? Get rid of the medical jargon and talk to them like a person! At my practice, we keep up to date with all the science and studies around regenerative medicine and stem cell therapy, but all of that information is not what is appealing to most people. What is appealing is telling them how those therapies can help them avoid surgery, get off pain meds, and return to the activities they love to do, without restrictions. I'm encouraging all of you to take off the white jacket for a minute, and talk to people like you would your own mother or child—with compassion, empathy, and a plan of care that speaks to the needs and desires of your patients. Take them on a journey, and show them what it will be like to do business with you.

Unf*cking Private Healthcare

This journey you are taking them on should be present on all your hard marketing materials. If you have rack cards or brochures or flyers, or send newsletters to your patients, you have to be able to speak to them about what it is like to do business with you. For example, if you treat back pain, don't use words like lumbar radiculopathy, spondylolisthesis, or lumbago, followed by a litany of scientific explanations of what all that shit is. No one cares, and it's over their heads, which means they won't read it. Talk to them about how the services you offer will help them get back to work or the sport they love. Tell them you understand the limits that back pain and sciatica (yes, people know this term) put on their lives. Advocate for people's health, and then talk about how your services can help them achieve their goal. This goes back to my empathy and authority discussion earlier. Tell people that back pain is the number 1 cause of missed work days in the United States, and your goal is to help them not be another statistic, by bringing nearly 15 years of experience in dealing with people who have suffered back injuries. Tell them that back pain doesn't have to be the reason they can't get up and down off the floor to play with their grandchildren. Let people know that you understand what they are going through, and how your expertise can help them.

At our regenerative medicine office, we don't "sell stem cells." We offer a better way of healing that helps people get off pain medicines, avoid surgery, and return to the things they love doing. It is a must that you market to your patients using language that they understand, empathy about what they may be going through, and how you plan to help them. Always use positivity, and pictures that show positive outcomes. Avoid using pictures of people in pain, as this will negatively impact their mindset. In Donald Miller's book, Building a Story Brand, he talks about how to use the essence of stories in your marketing. In every story, there is a hero and a guide. Stop trying to be the hero; that is someone else's story. Be their guide along the process. A patient or potential patient is the hero of their own story. You are not. As a healthcare provider, you are the guide. It is your job to show them a path that can lead them to success, and they must choose to take

www.thehealthcareplaybook.com

that path. Remember the AIDA acronym? You must walk them through these steps before they will trust you with the treatment plan you lay out for them.

Speaking of journeys, let's take a little journey through your office right now—through the eyes of a patient. Let's break down what they see, from the time they walk in the door to when they leave, as it relates to how you're marketing your services to them. We've discussed the lobby already, so I won't bust your balls anymore on that, but I do want to paint a picture for you.

It's a patient's first visit to your office. Your team has already done the discovery call and exuded great customer service and sales skills directly in line with the mission of the practice. As the patient steps in the door, they are greeted immediately by your welcome desk, and the steps we already discussed in the previous chapter take place. The patient goes to sit down and bang out their paperwork. This is the point where they will actually notice the setup of your lobby for the first time. What do they typically see? Usually some nice art on the wall, right? Why? Are we trying to appeal to their taste in art culture? Take that mess down, and put pictures of you and your team on the walls. Frame your vision and mission statements. If you have had the opportunity to take any pictures with famous or powerful people, put those up. Of course, these should be done tastefully, but nonetheless, the pictures on the wall should be a representation of the culture in your office.

As this patient takes a seat in your lobby, they may notice the absence of magazines or reading materials; but let's face it, most people look at their phones anyway. The money you spend on magazines is senseless. Instead, they have access to a patient testimonial book, where actual patients have written about their experiences in your office. This may seem a little dated to you, but contrary to common belief, not everyone has Google or social media, and not everyone is comfortable enough on camera to give you a video testimonial. Not

Unf*cking Private Healthcare

to mention there is a ton of power in the written word. A written testimonial actually demonstrates to other patients that someone was so pleased with their service and outcome that they wrote a message about it. This establishes more authority for you as the provider.

The coffee and end tables advertise your services in a way that speaks to the needs of the client. You have brochures about your ancillary services that attract people to want to learn more. The TV is actually showing your YouTube channel, or advertising some of your ancillary services. It even has testimonials scrolling on it. Again, your lobby is serving as a place where people are learning more about you before they have even seen you. You are establishing yourself as an expert and authority, and this patient may not have even made contact with you yet. Or maybe they have been seeing you for years and never realized the extra services you had to offer because you never showed them off.

When they are called back for their appointment, what do they see as they walk down the halls? What's hanging on the walls? When they eventually make it to their room, what do they see in there? Typically, it's framed posters of anatomy, and anatomy models sitting on the counters. Why? Why do we do this as healthcare providers? What class did you take that suggested this is the way to set up your treatment rooms? People don't read that shit, nor do they understand the jargon on those posters. Hell, I think I'm weird because I do read them; but again, I'm a healthcare provider. Put stuff on the walls that advocates for your services. You've already established your mission and vision statements as a part of this book, and we've already talked about sales strategies; so use what you know, and design a treatment room that speaks to your patients about themselves, not about you and your anatomy book.

When they filled out their paperwork back in the lobby, they should also have been given a health "check list" that asks questions directly in regard to your ancillary services, if you have them. An example of

www.thehealthcareplaybook.com

this would be a dermatologist having a questionnaire about skin care products that included questions about current products they use. Some questions you might include would be:

"Do you have questions about what products are the best for your skin?"

"Are you unsure about how you should be taking care of your skin on a daily basis?"

"Do you have questions about wrinkles?"

"Have you ever wanted to know more about Botox?"

"What's one thing about your skin you wish you could change?"

By asking these types of questions, you are framing a conversation to be had about your products and services. People don't know what they don't know, and if you can pull some interest out of them by asking questions, you will then have the opportunity to sell to them. Remember, marketing gets them interested and affords you the opportunity to sell. This checklist should be used by the medical assistant when they are taking the history, and then passed off to you as the provider. You would simply review the questionnaire with them after you have completed the reason for the appointment, and dive deeper into boxes marked "yes." People may not know that some over-the-counter skin care is bad for them, or that it dries your skin out. People don't know the value of the skin care you sell in your office until you open up a dialogue with them about it.

After you have spoken to them about their reason for coming in, provided a plan of care, and hopefully sold them on some of the ancillary products you have that will help them achieve their goals, they are escorted up to the follow-up desk (not the "check-out" desk), where they will be handed a welcome packet. This welcome packet

Unf*cking Private Healthcare

could be a folder or small bag that contains material in it that is actually useful. People like free shit. Our office provides a branded folder that has a welcome letter from our physician, a couple of brochures further talking about our ancillary products and services, a logo pen, any information they might need on a procedure they elected to have, and a printed sheet with QR codes, inviting them to follow us on social media, sign up for emails, and leave us a review. For a printable list of items you might think about including in your welcome packet, go to www.thehealthcareplaybook.com/booktools.

All in all, this type of signage, welcome packets, and advertising further goes to show your patients what you have to offer. It invites them to do more business with you, and potentially retains them as clients for more than just regular doctor's visits. Even more so, it begins a foundation of trust.

Think about this patient's experience in your office and what they saw. They weren't inundated with fluff and distractions. At every turn, they were advertised to, but not in a cheesy manner. Your office was set up to promote what you do, how you do it, and more importantly, why you do it. Remember in the early chapters of this book, where we discussed that people do business with your "why," way before they buy what you offer.

The follow-up after this appointment doesn't occur at their next appointment. It occurs that very same day via a handwritten letter from you, the provider. Yes, snail mail. Snail mail is largely neglected these days, which opens the door for you to separate yourself from everyone else. For every new patient you had for that day, you should sit down and handwrite a note to them. We use branded 5 x 7 postcards in bright blue envelopes for our practice. Bright blue because it is one of our brand colors, and also because it will stand out against all the white envelopes that everyone uses to mail you stuff. Our provider writes a short note thanking that particular patient for their time, and for trusting us with their health. Its looks something

www.thehealthcareplaybook.com

like this:

"Mrs. Jones, it was such a pleasure to meet you in our office today. Thank you for your time, and I hope we were respectful of it. I feel confident we can help you with your knee pain and get you back to training for that triathlon. One thing we know is that most people remember every question they didn't ask, after their appointment. If at any time this happens to you, and you have questions or concerns, please don't hesitate to contact our office.

P.S. The greatest compliment we could ever receive is a referral."

Signature.

You drop your business card in there, stamp it, and drop it in the mail. Hardly anyone does this. Remember 10–15 years ago, how much shit used to come to your mailbox? Piles and piles of nonsense that you mostly threw away. Now, however, there might be 3 pieces of mail in my box on a daily basis. When you send a letter via snail mail, it stands out to people. Hardly anyone writes letters anymore. Write the letter, and I guarantee you, it will stand out. This will go further to market your brand and what your office is all about.

On top of that, if you rely on referrals from other practitioners or lawyers for personal injury cases, Mrs. Jones is not the only one that gets a note. Whoever referred her gets one as well. It looks like this:

"Dr. Kevorkian, thank you so much for referring Mrs. Jones over to us for an evaluation of her knee. I feel confident we will be able to get her back to doing the things she loves. I appreciate your continued support of what we do at our office.

P.S. Please send more like her."

Signature

Unf*cking Private Healthcare

Quick. Simple. Respectful. When was the last time you referred someone to a colleague and they sent you a handwritten card in the mail thanking you? I bet your reaction would be, "Wow. That was nice of them to send that." This further solidifies your values and your brand, and markets you so very differently than anyone else.

Marketing doesn't have to be complicated. It just needs to deliver a message about your values, your mission, some empathy, and the change you hope to deliver to everyone that does business with you.

In the next chapter, we will start the discussion on digital platforms and how to use them in a similar fashion to your hard materials, with a few key points to remember. So, let's talk digital.

Chapter 7

Intro to Marketing – Digital Marketing

This is the chapter most of you are probably going to get the most out of when it comes to marketing. You undoubtedly have questions about how to do social media or why it's important. Or why your website isn't converting. Or why email marketing is significant, because you hate all the "marketing" emails you get every day. You've most likely paid someone to do your social media for you, but you have no idea how social media works or why it's important. You probably don't know how to measure its success. Or maybe you think social media is stupid, and you want nothing to do with it. Whatever your feelings are toward the digital marketing world, it's a necessary evil you must tap into in order to be noticed.

There is one key thing to remember when it comes to digital marketing, and this is especially true when it comes to social media. People want to know who you are, more so than what you do. Just like in previous chapters, we have talked about how nobody cares what you do until they know why you do it. In this chapter, we are going to talk about who you are and how to show people that. People identify with people. People relate to people with similar experiences, backgrounds, lifestyles, wins, and losses. Be relatable, and you will win in this world.

Let's talk about your website first, because your website needs to follow some of the same ideas we discussed in our hard marketing chapter. Disclaimer: I am not a website developer or expert on how

73

Unf*cking Private Healthcare

to construct a website. Nor do I give advice on SEO. There are experts for that. The tips I'm about to share with you are solely based upon better ways to market through your website by clearing up the messaging. Your website is essentially your digital brochure. A potential patient should be able to look at your website and in 5 seconds identify 3 things: what you offer, what problem you solve, and how to do business with you. People don't actually read websites. They scan through them. If you are unable to tell potential patients exactly what you do in a matter of seconds, they will move on to the next person down the street who has a clearer, more concise message. Most of you have websites that are confusing, use too much insider language (we talked about this is Chapter 6), and don't talk directly to the patient you are trying to attract.

The header on the home page of your website should be void of too much information that would confuse people of what they need to know about doing business with you. For example, there is often a list of menu items across the top of the page for people to choose from: "who we are; what we do; our services; what we treat; our story; about us; contact us," and so on and so forth. Why do we do this? Because so many other people do it that way. Let me tell you what those menu options actually do. They distract from what you want people to do. You want people to, "Call to schedule," or "Click here" to make an appointment; not read through 90 pages of content with medical jargon all over it, attempting to convince them that you are the best in your field before they make a decision. Let me clear up this one thing. You do not become the best in your field because you said it on your website. You become the best in your field because other people say it about you.

Make it simple—5th grade level of communication here. Put your logo in the upper left hand corner, a call to action (call now, click to schedule, etc.) in the upper right hand corner, and a picture of happy people, or a picture of you treating someone, dead center, with a short phrase that tells potential patients exactly what problem you solve;

and add one more call to action under those words. That's it. That's really all you need to show people when they first land on your webpage. Here is an example of what I'm talking about. The picture in this section is of a physical therapy practice I owned. You can see from the picture that it's obviously a physical therapy practice, because it says it in the title of the practice. You can see the unique piece of equipment we use that will undoubtedly provoke interest, you know exactly what to do to make an appointment, you know what makes us different, and most importantly, you can see how the words inspire a feeling. They inspire a feeling of restoration of their bodies, and personalization of their medical care.

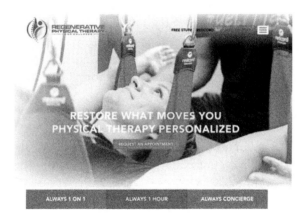

Let's refer back to the AIDA/R model of thinking. You have to capture attention, interest, desire, and action. How can you do that in the first 5 seconds if people are inundated with so much information that they can't grasp what you do, what problem you solve, or how to do business with you?

Let's also look at the top right corner where it says "Free stuff." If you want to grow as a practice, your website needs to add value to potential patients before they even schedule an appointment with you. In our "free stuff" section, we offer access to our blog and access to download free PDFs. These PDFs could be simple things like, "3 everyday things you can do to minimize back pain." Or, "Try these 5 exercises if your knee hurts when you go up and down steps." Whatever it is, it should be of value to your potential patients, and it should require an email address to get it. If it's not worth anything to your potential patient, it won't be worth giving an email address to get it. This is how you start building up your email marketing lists, which serves as yet another way to market to your potential patients. Omnipresence. Most healthcare practices only have email lists of current patients. This is okay, but these people only become a source of marketing that satisfies the "retention" part of our acronym, AIDA/R. What about the person that is interested but isn't quite sure if what you have is for them? You build value by adding "freebies" in exchange for an email address. You can then continue to nurture that person through email marketing. And yes, you are correct, you should have 2 separate email campaigns going to those 2 groups: those who have already done business with you, and those that haven't. The content for these groups is very different.

Before we talk about how those email campaigns are different, let me first squash a common bullshit belief I get all the time. This is what I hear: "I don't want to give away all this free stuff because then people won't feel the need to come and see me."

This is a fallacy. If you continue to give value to people, and build up a relationship of trust before they even step into your office, you will present yourself as an expert and an authority in their eyes. Besides, if you don't give them the information, someone else will. Ask yourself why you shouldn't be the one giving that value.

Now, for the 2 groups of emails. The first group of emails are your already established patients. These are people that (hopefully) already know, like, and trust you. These folks should get nurturing types of emails or offers/opportunities to purchase your ancillary services.

www.thehealthcareplaybook.com

They have already spent money for services in your practice, and therefore will be more likely to spend money at your practice again. For example, our regenerative medicine practice has specialty aesthetics procedures for hair loss, sexual dysfunction, and skin care; therefore, on a monthly basis, we will send out emails offering specials on these items. We may also advertise a new product, service, or device we just added to our arsenal. Now, assuming we have done a great job at servicing them in the past, they would be more likely to spend their money at our facility again.

The second group are your newbies. These are the people that have subscribed to your free stuff in exchange for an email address. These folks get value emails. Value emails are designed to do just what the title implies. They build value for the services and products you offer, or they demonstrate what doing business with you looks like. Value emails will have subject headings like:

"Here's what one of our clients is saying about us." Here is where you can show off a testimonial that someone gave you. This will further promote your expertise and authority.

"We used to think surgery was the only option. Not anymore..." This email is designed to show a paradigm shift. It gets people thinking more about why they should consider your product or service versus another. Or it serves to prime their mind to think differently about a certain product or service that their brains have been programmed to think otherwise about.

"You aren't sitting at home with knee pain, are you?" This is a problem + solution email. The problem is knee pain, and by opening the email, this particular patient will be shown your solution to their knee pain.

These types of value emails serve to build the relationship and establish a certain type of rapport that eventually leads them to doing business with you. Again, you are following the AIDA/R acronym of

Unf*cking Private Healthcare

getting attention, promoting interest, and eventually a desire to take action to get the benefit of the products and services you offer.

A third email list you might consider would be for potential or current referral sources. These are other doctors, healthcare providers, or attorneys (if you do personal injury) that need some nurturing and/or value propositioning. Talk to these people about why their clients/patients will be in good hands with you. Talk to them about outcomes your patients are getting by using the testimonial email. As I'm writing this book, we're in the middle of the 2020 Covid-19 pandemic, and going into other doctors' offices or lawyers' offices is tough to orchestrate, so I put together email campaigns offering to do video calls via Zoom, GoToMeeting, FaceTime, etc. This shows that I care about the relationship and am willing to do things that maintain that relationship during critical, limited social times.

Other items and guidelines for your emails are:

Always add a call to action (CTA). What do you want people to do with the information you are giving them? Call to get the deal? Schedule an appointment? Buy now? Many of these email campaign platforms will allow you to put an action button in the email and link it to the particular call to action. USE IT!

Links to social media. You need these on your email. Invite people to connect with all your platforms. Put a CTA that says, "Click the links below to follow us on social media."

Minimal pictures. This is a big one for me. Don't inundate your people with pictures. It's an email, not an encyclopedia of pictograms. Put words in it! Research will tell you that people are more likely to read words than scroll through a litany of pictures.

Short in length. Keep your emails short. If people have to scroll for days on end in order for you to land your plane of thought, they will

www.thehealthcareplaybook.com

delete it, unsubscribe from it, and move the fuck on.

Be interesting and relatable. You don't have to be a comedian or scientist, or in this case, a doctor. Talk to people about what you have and why they need it in their lives. Relate to everyday struggles with knee pain, loss of confidence due to bad skin, being a mom, having reflux, etc. Tell them how doing business with you will make their lives better.

Add a P.S. For some strange reason, this works. Some people will read the beginning and the end of your email, but not the body of it. Adding a P.S. with a fun fact and CTA works well.

And last but not least, when it comes to email marketing, most of you want to know how often you should send them. The minimum is once a week, but honestly, if you went to the gym just once a week, would you see much change? That's obviously a rhetorical question.

"But Trib, won't people unsubscribe if I send them too many emails?" Maybe; however, they are more likely to forget you exist if you don't send multiple emails per week. Personally, daily is a bit much for me, but a good rule of thumb that I recommend is 3 per week to each group on your list. If you're interesting and relatable, they won't unsubscribe from your list.

Now that our email tangent is complete, let's get back to the website. If you were to continue to scroll down the page I shared with you earlier, you would see continued value- building and important empathy-authority types of statements. Statements like: "Pain is frustrating and limits your life."

"Renew the confidence in your body."

"Our physical therapists have specialized training to help people just like you overcome back and joint pain."

These are accompanied with photos of people doing therapy in our facility, along with certain conditions we treat. If they are actively searching for a physical therapist, GI practice, or OB/GYN, there is no need to tell them all about the WHAT. They already know what they're looking for. You simply need to talk to them about themselves, and speak to how you want to help them achieve their goals. Stop with the cornucopia of language that people don't identify with; and more importantly, stop telling people about how great you are. It drives me nuts when I see people use tag lines like, "When it comes to (insert specialty), we're your best bet." Why? Because you said so? Talk about how they will feel after doing business with you. Create a story, with them as the main character, not you.

Remember the 3-step chart we identified earlier? The 3-step process of making the intangible, tangible? This can also show up on your website. You have to tell people what to do or they won't do it. Hold their hand on your website, and walk them through your process so they know exactly what to expect. Take that 3-step process and put it right there on your homepage. Here's what it looks like on our physical therapy website.

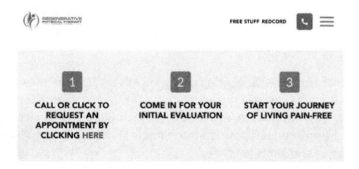

Notice how simple this looks and how easy it makes people understand how to do business with you. Hold their hand, tell them what to do, and walk them through it.

www.thehealthcareplaybook.com

Lastly, and certainly not least, your website should link to all your social media accounts. It should invite people to connect with you on all of them: Twitter, Facebook, Instagram, Snapchat, YouTube, TikTok, LinkedIn, your Podcast, etc. This also means you should have a presence on multiple social media platforms. And here comes the argument, and believe me, I've heard them all. Listen, I don't care if you don't like social media, don't believe in social media, don't want to understand it, think it's too complicated, don't understand the algorithms (nobody does)—whatever your excuse is, get over it. This is FREE marketing for you and your business. I'll repeat it: FREE marketing. You need to have a presence on social media. At one point in time, you didn't know shit about the specialty in the medical field you wanted to go into. You learned it. Just like then, you have to learn this now.

Did you know that the fastest growing population of people on Facebook are those over the age of 60? Did you know that as a whole, the majority of millennials do business via social media? Did you know that recent research indicates that 50% of Americans listen to Podcasts? This is extraordinary. If you have valuable content to offer, you can reach a large volume of people while they drive or workout. If you want to stand out, you must be active on these platforms. And by active, I mean you need to be on them just like the number of meals you eat in a day. Breakfast, lunch, and dinner. Yes, at least 3 times per day on each platform. I know it sounds like a lot, but there are social media calendar platforms out there that can automate and compile your posting into one area. You can build up your content, and the system will automatically post them at the desired times you select. Just go to your favorite internet search engine, and look up social media automation tools.

Your next question will be, what are the best times to post? Well, I mentioned breakfast, lunch, and dinner. You should be active on your social media in the mornings, usually around 8/8:30am; then again during lunch, 11:30–1pm; right at the end of the work day, around

Unf*cking Private Healthcare

4:30/5 pm; and if you like, again later in the evening, around 7:30pm works well also. These times are relatively strategic because most of the insight on social media suggests that people will check their social media accounts right when they get to work or after getting the kids off to school, during their lunch hour, right at the end of the day before they punch out, and one more time at the end of the evening, after dinner and right before bed. If you're active during these times, you have a higher likelihood of getting noticed and seen. You can also go into the menus on your social media and search through the analytics to see what days and times you're getting the most attention.

The biggest pet peeve I have with healthcare practices is their engagement on social media. Remember, this is "social" media. You have to be social. You can't just get on there, post a picture, and be done. Nor can you post a picture with one sentence in the caption, and mic drop your way out. Your caption has to invite people into a conversation and promote engagement. Don't be afraid to ask people to comment. Don't be afraid to search for people with similar specialties and comment on their stuff. Better yet, reply to people that have commented on other healthcare practices' posts, and engage with them. Find trending topics, and use them in your posts to get noticed. Again, be social and interact!

As far as your caption goes, this is an area where I see healthcare providers fail miserably with insider language. Most of you have a tendency to get on there and use big medical language, which doesn't attract consumers because they don't understand it. Stop using language like, "Today, I performed a 3-level laminectomy/discectomy on a patient with multiple broad based disc protrusions at L3-S1. They had radicular symptoms down both legs. If this sounds like you, I can help."

It's ridiculous, and it doesn't speak to the person or persons who actually have a back problem. It may attract other healthcare providers, whom are less likely to generate leads for you. They may

www.thehealthcareplaybook.com

"like" your content, but they aren't going to actively seek out your services. Dumb down the language. Speak in layman's terms. Use relatable content, and be funny, quirky, silly, dry, serious, etc. if that's your personality. Tell people more about who you are versus what you are doing. Not every post has to be a procedure you did or some scientific breakthrough. Let's take our same sentence from earlier, and I'll translate it for you in a way that it will draw people in without sounding pretentious.

"Back pain and sciatica, which is when you have pain, burning, or tingling down your leg/s, can be such a debilitating situation. It can affect your ability to work, provide for your family, and enjoy everyday life. As a spine surgeon, I understand how depressing it is to feel like there's no hope. Surgery isn't the only way to fix your problem, but at times there is little to no other choice. Today, I did a pretty big surgery on a person who has had several years of back pain and had tried everything from injections to physical therapy, without relief. We're hoping, after this surgery, he will be able to get back to doing the things he loves, and we will be cheering him on along the way. If you or someone you know has debilitating back pain, I encourage you to reach out to us. Check the link in our bio, and get your free PDF of my top-5 recommendations for helping back pain."

This caption speaks to people. It doesn't announce your big egotistical brain. It shows empathy and then invites people to take action; and when they do, they get something for free. You are showing people you care, rather than showing off your skill set. This will win 100% (well, maybe 99.9%) of the time. Be authentic and caring, and you will stand out.

Take time to post about your team. Show pictures of your office. Share wins. For example, if one of your team members gets a new certification, announces an engagement or a pregnancy, took a cool trip, met a weight loss goal, etc., post about it. Post a picture of the birthday girl holding a cake, or a video of your team singing to him or

Unf*cking Private Healthcare

her. Post a Halloween picture if your team dressed up. Advocating for your team, and celebrating their wins, shows people your culture. Just make sure your team consents to you posting about them first.

As the provider, you should already be a celebrity in your patients' eyes before they even walk in your clinic. Post pics of what you did over the weekend. If you're a parent, show yourself doing activities with your kids (if you feel comfortable). This will speak to those who are also parents. If you're a golfer, gym rat, or pickle ball player, post about it. These are things that people will relate to outside of the daily grind. I promise you, if you show people more about who you are, you will attract so much more attention on social media. You will become relatable as a person, which means more to people than your profession.

A word of warning when it comes to social media: Each platform is different. Be sure you understand the audience on each one, and make your content specific to the person you want to attract. For instance, I mentioned that Facebook has a larger over-60 population, so you would gear your content toward that demographic. We're a regenerative medicine practice, which means a lot of our clients are over 40 years old, so we get more attention on Facebook for those services than on Instagram. Instagram and Snapchat have a younger, more millennial population, so you may want to shift your content to appeal to millennials. This is why our aesthetics services do better on Instagram. In my experience, LinkedIn and Twitter tend to be a little more business to business connections rather than business to consumer. You can be a little more scientific on these platforms and use your insider language. A short one liner post on Twitter will typically not perform as well on Instagram or Facebook. Why do I tell you that? Because you don't want to blanket post across these platforms. Make your content and captions specific to each platform. It's really tempting to copy and paste it all, but the reception is not the same across the individual platforms.

www.thehealthcareplaybook.com

Promoted posts or "boosted" posts to reach a wider audience is a great thing that some of these platforms offer; however, you need to know what you are doing here. Make no mistake, these platforms will take your money regardless of how well you do this. They are also a business. If you blanket a large area with very general specifics about who you want to reach, paid promotions will not do well for you. You must learn to target a specific audience with your content. For instance, if you are an OB/GYN practice, you wouldn't want to do a paid promotional post to men and women, ages 18–65. That would make no sense. You would want to dial in on women between the ages of 25 and 40, with a specific radius to your geographic location. You would also want to find certain interest profiles that these people might be a part of, such as moms groups, maternity classes, baby clothes, etc. Targeting specific people with specific interests, in a specific location, will improve your chances of getting engagement. Again, you need to familiarize yourself with how to do this, or make sure you have a social media marketer that knows what the hell they are doing.

Hashtags, or the pound sign, for those of you who have more candles on the birthday cake, are great tools to use. Hashtags are keywords or keyword phrases with the number sign (#) in front of them. They can be used anywhere in the caption of your post—beginning, middle, or end. They identify with a certain topic, and help other users find content with that specific topic or theme. These topics or hashtags are searchable, which is why you want the topics you discuss to have them. Hashtags are a great way to attract new followers with interest in what you're talking about. Again, there are certain parameters you would want to follow when using them. Two of the biggest things I see people neglect to do is add a geographical hashtag and a company hashtag. I'll explain. Let's say your office is in Dallas, TX, and on any given day, you have 100 likes on your posts, but the majority of those people "liking" your posts are in California. These people will be less likely to become your patients, for obvious reasons. Using #dallas will help people in your immediate area find your services. The second is

Unf*cking Private Healthcare

making your own hashtag from your company name. For example, if I owned a spine center, I might start using #TribbySpineCenter, and I would put that hashtag on my business card, and ask anyone who left us a review on social media to use it as well. This helps group the posts about your practice into one place where people can consume the content relevant to your practice. This is really beneficial if you have multiple providers working in the same practice, and who have individual doctor pages, which they should have. This will all increase your chances of being noticed.

I could go on and on about social media and, in fact, could probably write another 10- chapter book on digital marketing alone. Maybe I will. Stay tuned. There are multiple different hashtags you could use with very different ways to use them: how to do the correct paid promotions; "stories" on Facebook and Instagram; filters; going "Live," doing videos; knowing how to decipher your analytics and use them to reach the right people; how to find what is trending and use it; and on and on. There is so much stuff to consider, which is why a lot of you feel it's daunting and often hire someone else to do your digital marketing. The only problem is that most people that do digital marketing don't have a healthcare background and often don't understand the language, which means you constantly have to monitor it and make sure they're saying the right things. Luckily, I feel your pain. I get it because I've been there, which is why I spent time learning how to do all of this. I no longer have to explain to the marketer how to post about regenerative medicine. If you need some social media guidance, I'd love to talk more about it with you. You can get in touch with me at www.thehealthcareplaybook.com. You can also find a printable hard and digital marketing checklist for your use.

Hopefully this chapter has given you a look into the digital world but has also helped you see why the digital world is so important and why you need to be a part of it. All of your hard marketing collateral should link to your digital platforms. Give people the chance to get to know you on these digital platforms. Use QR codes to direct people to them.

www.thehealthcareplaybook.com

A QR code, or quick response code, is a barcode that people can scan with their smartphones. Again, go to your trusty search engine and look for QR code generators, and you will be treated to a plethora of companies that do this. I make sure to develop QR codes for all the practices I work with, so that clients have one code to scan that leads to all their digital platforms. Guess where this also goes? Yes, your business card. Making things simple for people to interact with you is the way to go.

Let's recap. You've established new messaging, new mission and vision statements, new leadership skills, better customer service and sales strategies, and have fixed your marketing funnels. This is all leading to more satisfied customers and, undoubtedly, more money for your practice. So what are you going to do with all that money? That's what we are going to cover next. How do you adequately manage the profits of your practice? Get ready to tap into your inner accountant—another subject many of you didn't get a degree in and, therefore, are not financially literate. I wasn't either, and it was painful to learn what I'm about to share with you.

Chapter 8

Financials –The Dreaded Money Chapter

Oh, the dreaded discussion about money and how to manage it. I'm making the assumption here that most of you love accounting so much that you hire someone else to do it. Or maybe you're fumbling through spreadsheets every month, trying to keep it all together yourself. Managing personal expenses is something that most of us are already bad at, but now we have to manage the money for a business. This is a totally different animal to deal with, and this animal can have sharp teeth. Another disclaimer: I am not a financial advisor, nor am I an accountant. I am only sharing tips with you that have helped me learn how to better manage money. It is 100% up to you to decide if these things are right for you, and whether or not you should seek guidance from your financial advisors or accountants on these matters. If you don't have an accountant, now would be the time to get one.

We could agree that the majority of Americans work paycheck to paycheck. There is a saying that the average American is 3 missed paychecks from bankruptcy. What about your business or your practice? How close are you to not being able to pay the bills? How much money should you have in reserve to float your practice in an economic crisis? It's 2020, and we're in the middle of a pandemic. Did this affect you financially? Maybe it was a Wednesday, and payroll was about to go out on Friday, and you noticed that you didn't have the funds. Shit, now what do you do? Have you ever had to call in a favor to make payroll or cover the bills? I certainly have. It sucks, and no matter what, that bill train is always on time.

What about taxes? How do you make sure you have enough money to pay Uncle Sam his percent? If your overhead is 60–70%, like most healthcare practices, that only leaves 30–40% in actual revenue. While there are perks to owning a business when it comes to taxes, how do you ensure you have enough to pay what you do owe? How do you cut down on the high overhead? If you're profitable, what should you actually do with those profits?

Have you ever heard the saying, "Pay yourself first?" What does that even mean, and how do you do that? Why is it important to pay yourself first, even if it's a small amount? These are all subjects we will touch on in this chapter. My hope is that you will have a clearer understanding of how to manage your business finances, and that knowledge potentially flows into your personal financial life.

I believe that a lot of healthcare providers go through a ton of school, end up with a mound of student loans, and desire to open their own practices so they can, "be their own boss," but nevertheless, that first big paycheck or profitable month comes, and you spend that money on a nice new car or a home in a country club. Why? The answer is that it's a status thing, and you think you deserve it after all the school you just went through. Don't get me wrong; it's great to have nice things. Hell, I like having nice things, but most of you feel that because you are a doctor or a business owner, you need to have these things in your personal life to look the part; however, all these material items do is put a strain on your business if you don't have the proper money management system in place.

It's time to get out of the mindset of being a healthcare professional, and into the mindset of being a business owner. Being a business owner means you have to be financially literate. You have to be able to read the numbers and understand how the money coming in and out of your practice works, and how to make that money work for you.

www.thehealthcareplaybook.com

Gone are the days where you worked for another practice as an employee. You are currently moving into the self-employed spectrum of the job world, and you cannot make it to the business owner or entrepreneur world until you learn how to manage the money or at least put systems in place to manage it. Most of you will work 70+ hours a week to make your dream happen, which is fine because you have to manage the business and manage a patient load. In the long run, if you want to become a true business owner, you have to learn to focus on the business and let others work for you. A large part of getting to this point is improving your financial literacy.

First step, get an accountant if you don't have one. If you don't have a good one, get a new one. These people are trained to look at spreadsheets and show you where your money goes. If you have a good one, then you should be having, at a minimum, quarterly meetings (preferably monthly) with them to discuss the numbers. The items that you need to know each quarter are:

1. What were the expenses? Break them down into 2 groups.

Group 1: Subcontractors/rentals. This group is essentially anyone that is not on your payroll, or any equipment you don't own. So, if you outsource your billing, have a CPA, legal fees, use a CRNA for in-house procedures, rental equipment, etc., this is where these expenses live.

Group 2: Operating expenses. This is your payroll, rent, utilities, office supplies, any capital equipment you purchased this quarter, etc. These are your monthly reoccurring expenses.

2. What was the revenue? Actual revenue is not the total amount of money you brought in. Actual revenue, as I am defining in this book, will be the amount you brought in after you paid for your expense group 1. Why? Because the subcontractors you use have to be paid first. You never really see that money or have true control over using it in your business.

Unf*cking Private Healthcare

3. What are the potential estimated taxes? You should be paying quarterly estimates when possible, in order to stay ahead and keep you from paying a large lump of taxes you may owe at the end of the year. This is where your CPA is your friend and can help you determine those amounts.

4. What were your profits (if any)?

Profit is the money you actually have in the bank after all operating expenses are paid, your salary is paid, and the taxes are separated. Cash is king, and you should be wanting to see the profit column grow. I'll talk about how to do this shortly.

Many of you may already be doing these meetings with your CPA on a regular basis, and your CPA will often show you that you have made a profit; but you, as the business owner, will think, "Hmm, where did that money go?" Sound familiar? It's kind of like going to the grocery store for 1 or 2 things, and leaving with $200 worth of shit. Yeah, it happens like that in business as well. The reason is that we often suck at organizing our cash flow to see where it goes. We just spend it from the same 1 or 2 accounts. This is why I firmly believe you should have 4 or 5 business accounts at your bank, to help you manage your money. I'll explain.

Most of you check your business bank account regularly, and everything you spend comes from one account. You're constantly monitoring that one account—every deposit and every check that you write. You probably even decide which bills take priority month to month, and pay those first, hoping you have enough for say the cable/Wi-Fi bill at the end of the month. As long as there is money there, you feel good about it. You stress daily over what the numbers in that account say. This is a habit that's hard to break and, therefore, rather than change the habit, let's improve the functionality of that habit.

www.thehealthcareplaybook.com

You should have multiple bank accounts to split your revenue into. Here's a good way to do it. Create 5 separate accounts that are titled: revenue, expenses, profit, taxes, and owner's pay. You should be able to go into your online banking accounts and rename the accounts, as I listed above, to make moving the money around easy. Every dollar the business earns gets deposited into the revenue account. From there, you will split each dollar by a percentage into these various accounts. The idea behind this is to make sure you are paying yourself and your business every month, setting aside adequate money for taxes, and also putting a set amount into the expenses bucket. The set amount into the expenses account is to help you keep your expenses under that amount.

A historian named C. Northcote Parkinson came up with the idea or principle, which later became coined as Parkinson's Law, and it states that people will use the maximum amount of time in a work day to complete a task or series of tasks. In other words, if you are given 8 hours to complete a task, you will use those 8 hours to accomplish it. If you were given 3 days to complete the same task, chances are you would use those 3 days. If you apply this principle to money in your business, it works the same way. In Mike Michalowicz's book, Profit First, which I recommend reading, he applies Parkinson's Law in the following manner: If you are given $10,000 dollars to complete a job, you will use exactly that amount to get the job done, but if given $1,000 dollars to complete the same job, you would also make it happen with $1,000. Apply this same logic to your expenses. Chances are, if you have access to $100,000 dollars every month in a single account, you will spend it. And most of the time, you will spend it on shit you don't even need. Hence, the reason you sit in front of your accountant who says you were profitable this year, and you think, "Hmm, where the hell did the money go?"

You need to have an expense account that forces you to keep your expenses under a certain amount. Some of you are just spending money because it's available, and not actually being innovative in

Unf*cking Private Healthcare

areas where you can, or going without when you can. Here's the clincher: You are not allowed to spend all the money in your expense account and then go borrow from another account such as your tax account.

So, how much money should you put in your expense account each month? That depends on how big your practice is. A medical business is not like any other business, especially as a sole practitioner. The main reason is because there is a need for support staff. A lot of general sole proprietors or self-employed people only have one employee—themselves—so they may only have 30% or less overhead, and can take 50% of the money they make as a salary. In a medical office with a sole provider, you still need someone to answer phones and schedule appointments, someone to do your billing, and a medical assistant. The need for support staff increases with the addition of providers and volume of patients.

If you are a small practice and a sole practitioner, meaning you are the only provider, a good target for expenses is 50%. If you are a medium-size practice with 2–5 providers, I would take the target up to 55%. If you are a larger practice of 5–10 providers, your target expenses percentage should be 60%. And if you have more than 10 practitioners, your expenses are more than likely close to 65%. The main reason this happens is because, as the number of providers you have increases, so does the need for a larger space (or multiple spaces), more staff, more equipment, and larger budgets for marketing, training, etc.

Keep in mind that these are targets. Many of you are probably over these targets and need to ask yourself where you can cut expenses. Make Parkinson's Law work for you. Can you get the same job done with 5% less money available in the expense account? The answer most likely is yes. The reality is usually that you don't want to because that puts more work on you, or there is an emotional response to staff cutbacks, but if you want to become a successful business owner, then

www.thehealthcareplaybook.com

you need to start paying attention to where the money goes, particularly in the expense column. Some of the most costly things to consider looking into are payroll taxes, health insurance plans for your employees, merchant costs, and your medical liability insurance. Many of you will try to offset your expenses by increasing your volume of patients. I caution you against doing this because it will have a direct impact on your customer service and sales strategies we talked about earlier in this book. Start looking internally at what you can change, rather than externally to compete against your spending issue.

When you have your expense target locked in, it's now time to discuss the remaining percentages and how to allocate them. First, let's look at your salary as an owner. Yes, you should be taking a regular salary, no matter how small or insignificant you think it is. You've all heard the saying (or at least I hope you have), "Pay yourself first." Please get into the habit of doing this. Paying yourself first, works 2 ways: You pay yourself as an individual, and you pay your business.

You are the one that started this business. Why would you pay yourself last? You start a business, work your butt off, pay all the bills, and have nothing left for yourself. Why? Pay yourself first. If you're thinking that you can't because your expenses are too high, please go back and read the last few paragraphs again. You have to learn to make your business thrive on less expenditures so you can pay yourself. As the owner of a sole practitioner office, your target for your own salary should be 30% of the revenue you generate. If you have 2–5 providers/owners, 25% is shared between those providers. If for some crazy-ass reason, you have 5–10 providers with ownership in the business, they will share 20% of the revenue as salary. And dear God, I hope you don't have more than 10 owners in your practice, because that's a lot of ego to manage; but if you do, you will need to share a salary of 15% of the revenue. The reason this drops as the number of owners increases, is because the more providers you have, the more money you make, which means there is more to share; however, there are also more expenses. In every case, this will leave you with about 20% of revenue,

Unf*cking Private Healthcare

which will then be split between the profit and tax accounts.

Once you have figured out your percentage for the owner or owners of the practice, you will then pay yourself first again. What do I mean? It's simple. Take 9/10 of your pay to live off of, pay bills, buy food and clothes, etc., and keep 1/10 in a separate account for saving and investing. I won't get into the specifics of how to go about saving money and investing money, but I will tell you that there are a lot of you as healthcare providers who are still living paycheck to paycheck, regardless as to how much money you make. You purchase big homes and nice cars, and work yourself into debt, thinking that all your toys are assets. Tip: Your home is not your asset. It's your liability. Your home is the bank's asset. Start educating yourself on better assets in order to make the money you earn work for you. It is not government backed retirement funds, or the savings account at your bank that offers you a whopping 1.6%, that will make you wealthy. Educate yourself on smart personal financial decisions that keep paying you as time goes on.

Paying your business first is also important. A percentage of the revenue you make each month should go into the account labeled profit. This will ensure you have cash on hand, and will protect the growth of the business as a whole. Remember that cash is king. If you have aspirations of one day selling your business, profitability is what will be considered in the valuation of the sale. Knowing that, why wouldn't you want to feed that account? Every month, you will move 10% of your revenue into the profit account, and there it will live. You are not allowed to borrow from this account. The temptation will be to use this money to help when expenses get high. I hate to break it to you, but the problem is not the expense column. It's the bad habits of you, the business owner, forcing the expense column higher. Fix your spending, and don't borrow from the profit account. If it helps, put the profit account at a separate bank so that you're not tempted to transfer between accounts within the same bank electronically. The profit account should always, at a minimum, have enough cash on

www.thehealthcareplaybook.com

hand to float your business for 3 months. Think about how great that little gem is during the time of the Covid-19 pandemic. How many of you had to take government bail outs to make it through that? Or cut your own salary? Or trim your staff down? If you had been paying your business first, you may have had much less stress during that.

So, what do you do with the money in your profit account, other than just make sure you have 3 months' worth of expenses in it at all times? Spend that shit! But spend in a specific way. Every quarter, you will take 50% of the money in the profit account as a disbursement to the owners. Each owner gets their share of the pie, of the money earned that quarter, depending on the percentage of the business owned. This is the time when being a business owner truly pays off. Take a trip, buy the car or the house you've been eye balling, or preferably, pay off some debt, but always remember to pay yourself 1/10 to your investments or assets, so that you can continue to make money work for you. The other 50% continues to live in the profit account to support the business. At the end of the year, after you've taken your 4th quarter disbursement, use the money in the profit account to expand your business if you like. Buy the new piece of equipment you've been wanting, or move to a new location, or hire more people, or pay off your business loans and debts, or maybe give your staff a yearly bonus from it. Whatever it is, this is the time to do it, and to do it without making more debt for your business. Use the cash on hand that has been living in the profit account to expand the business. I'm not saying spend all of it. Be reasonable with what you spend it on, and always remember to keep, at a minimum, 3 months of expenses in that account.

Here is the main rule: When cash is high, buy. When cash is low, lease or rent. Too many of you are wanting the newest, shiniest things when you first open your business, and you spend hundreds of thousands of dollars on these things when you simply don't need them. This drives you further into debt, and you haven't even seen a single patient yet. Be smart with the money you spend on your practice. It

Unf*cking Private Healthcare

makes no sense to work endlessly to pay off growing debts for your practice, and have zero dollars for your practice to thrive off of. You don't want to be the 65-year-old healthcare provider that can't retire because they have built a mountain of debt around their business and personal life. These are the ones that have put aside money for their kid's college fund, or that new house or that new toy for their office, and when all of that is paid for, they realize they haven't saved or haven't grown their own asset column. They have to keep working in order to live, because they have nothing to retire on.

Last but not least is Uncle Sam's account—the tax account—the one we most look forward to every year, and the one that chaps our asses. Fortunately, as a healthcare business owner, you do have a great amount of tax breaks as compared to being an employee; however, those checks are still painful to write. Please make sure you are using an accountant for this. Again, I am not an accountant, and I have no clue what you should or shouldn't be paying in taxes for your business, or deductions you qualify for. I do know that many of you are scrounging, come April, to scrape the cash together to pay your taxes. Why do you do that? Simple: No one has told you to make sure you allocate 10% of every dollar you make to the tax account, and then, every quarter, work with your accountant to find out what your estimated taxes are, and pay them. Yes, 10%. The typical business should be setting aside 15% each month for taxes; however, as a healthcare practice, this is where your high expenses actually provide an advantage. Your expenses serve as a significant write-off to your tax bill. And no, that is not permission to run your expenses higher! Tip: Don't wait until April or October (if you filed for an extension) to pay your taxes. That money sitting in the tax account will be way too tempting to use. Pay them quarterly. And guess what? If you happen to over pay during the year, and you get a return or there is money left over in the tax account, you get another bonus! Queue the ticker tape parade.

www.thehealthcareplaybook.com

We have now gone through how to separate each dollar earned into a money management system; and believe me, it works. I know some of you may have looked at the percentages I suggested, and thought, "Yeah. There's no way!" I get it. I've thought that as well. Here's a tip: Don't start with the percentages I gave you; work your way toward them. I realize this type of system will be different and will be an adjustment, so start with allocating 1 or 2% to some of these accounts in the beginning, just to get into the habit. As your practice grows and you find ways to bring the expenses down, you can begin to up the percentages until you're where you should be. Adjust them as you go. Maybe you are good with throwing 12% into your profit account because you have a great handle on your expenses. Maybe you need to do 12% to your taxes because your state laws are different. What I am giving you is more of a mindset change, and guidelines to a simple method you can use to better manage the money in your business. It's up to you to decide how to make these things work best for your practice and your particular situation.

Alright, I have shared some key skills in the last 8 chapters, and now it's time to put them all together. From core values and leadership, to mission and vision statements, to supreme customer service, to great sales and marketing, to being an awesome money manager—these are skills you need to develop in order to make the transition to being a true business owner. Make no mistake; it's not easy to make some of these changes, and it takes time and dedication to implement these things. Let's talk about how to go about making these changes.

Chapter 9

Putting It All Together

Over the last 8 chapters, we have talked about a lot of topics within your business. A lot of these topics were things you may or may not have learned about along the way. Like I have said multiple times already, healthcare providers are one skill away from truly being great business owners. Have the honest conversation with yourself about which of these things is your kryptonite. Maybe it's more than one. The biggest thing I have to say on that subject is that it is okay. Pick one thing and start there. Trying to change everything, and learn about everything I mentioned in this book all at once, will be overwhelming and make you likely to say, "Fuck it." Pick one thing and get really good at it. Then go to the next thing. Small incremental changes is what will get you there. More importantly, it will keep you sane. As healthcare providers, we already juggle so many different things, from our staff to our patients, to being on call and trying to manage a family. Take the small steps necessary to be a better leader and better business owner, and work won't actually feel like work anymore.

The first step is deciding to make the change. Everything I have shared with you is designed to be a contribution, not a criticism. The same will be said about the 1-on-1 meetings with your team. Find out what their contributing ideas are, and don't take them as criticism. Take them as an opportunity to learn more about yourself as a business owner, a leader, and as a person. I have also had to look back at decisions I made as a business owner and leader, and many times I've realized I've made some bad choices. The difference between being a

Unf*cking Private Healthcare

bad business owner and a good one, is not about making all the right decisions. It's realizing when you make wrong ones, owning them, and relying on your team and those close to you to help you get better. Everything happens because of you, not to you.

Make a decision to move forward with something better—something you, your team, and your patients deserve—or you are making the conscious decision to stay the same. Remember, the way it has always been done is where innovation goes to die. Take steps to improve your practice by discovering (or rediscovering) why you got into being a business owner. Find out why you may or may not be good at owning your business.

Find out what it is your team wants when they come to work. What are their goals and aspirations? Share yours with them. What are they looking for? Use it to motivate yourself and them. When you put patient care and customer service second to your team culture, you achieve great things. That is not to say your patients are not important. It means that you can't adequately service your patients until you are servicing your team and your business. These are your beginning steps to defining yourself as a leader. You must have vision to lead people to a place they can't see.

Decide that you want more for your business, your team, and your patients than the status quo that has become healthcare. Decide to be better a leader. Decide to develop mission and vision statements. Decide to take a leadership course. Decide to learn more about sales and customer service. Decide to learn why proper marketing is vital to your success. Decide to get the finances under control and put your money to work for you. Decide that you are going to do what it takes to stand out and be noticed for who you are and why you do what you do, and let the "what" fall into place. Most of you are overwhelmed and feel unsatisfied because you focus on the WHAT and not the WHY.

www.thehealthcareplaybook.com

In order to find your why and put it into place, you will need to decide what it is you are all about. Are you about being normal and swimming in what Raymond Aaron calls the "sea of sameness?" Or are you about being extraordinary, and separating yourself from what everyone else does? So what are you all about?

I am about growth—growth as a person and as a business owner. I'm about helping my team accomplish their goals as people and as professionals. I'm about creating better systems for my practice so that it runs smoother. I'm about treating patients with empathy and with the desire to help them reach their goals. It drives me absolutely crazy when I walk into a healthcare practice for my own appointment, or one for my son, and am met with the same shitty experience and customer service the majority of these practices offer. It happens over and over again, and it has become a motivator for what not to be as a business owner. Every day, I make it a goal to compete with myself from the day before. Am I getting better as a person each day? Am I getting better as a business owner? I don't compete against other practices in my area. I compete against myself, and that is what will ultimately make our practice stand out.

So ask yourself if you're ready to separate yourself from that sea of sameness. What is it that you are all about, for your team, your business, your patients, and your future as a healthcare practice owner? Write these things down. In fact, you should have all of your goals and ideas written down. I have 2 very large dry erase boards in my home office that serve as vision boards. These are not just pipe dream boards where I write down ostentatious, unrealistic shit. These serve as a strategic way to put the things I want in clear sight, and allow me to write down action items that lead me directly to each one of those goals or dreams. How do you think this book got written?

Here's how you do it. At the top of your board, write your big goal: your 25-year goal from right now, or less if you don't plan to stay in healthcare for 25 more years. What do you want to see happen to

Unf*cking Private Healthcare

your practice or business, 25 years from now? This goal should feel a little out of reach and slightly unattainable; if it's not, it's too easy, and you'll find yourself not completely satisfied when you get there. It has to drive you every day to put the work in to get there. Something like, "Sell my practice for 500 million dollars and retire in the mountains with my family."

The next line will be your 10-year goal. Where do you want to be, 10 years from right now? These are the things that need to happen, from now and for the next 10 years, that will feed right into your big goal. I would put 3–5 things in this section. Examples would be:

1. Have 5 centers running at 85% productivity or more.

2. Each center has 5 full-time providers, and I am no longer treating.

3. Each center brings in 10 million dollars in gross revenue/year.

4. At least 20% of our revenue is from ancillaries.

5. Customer service satisfaction is above 90%.

Yes, I realize these numbers may not be representative of what you want or what you have experienced. I am using them solely as examples of what to include on your board.

The next section is your 5-year goal. Where do you want to be in the next 5 years? Write those 3–5 goals down. These goals should feed into your 10-year goals. Again, 3–5 bullet points.

1. Have 2 centers running at 85% productivity while looking for a 3rd location.

2. Each center generates 8 million dollars in gross revenue.

www.thehealthcareplaybook.com

3. I am only treating patients 3 days a week.

4. Ancillaries account for 20% of the revenue.

5. Customer service satisfaction is about 90%.

Lastly, you will break down your 5-year goals. Do the same 3–5 bullet points that you want to see happen at the 5-year mark. Then take it down to one year at a time, starting with the next year. What are the things you need to accomplish in the next 12 months that will directly feed into your 5-year plan? Break these down by quarters. List them out, starting with Q1, then move to Q2, and so on and so forth. Make these actionable items with time lines attached to them. Include new systems you need to put into place, leadership courses or business courses you may need to attend, CME courses, new trainings for your team, new hire plans, new ancillaries you want to add, etc. It is very important that you make an outline of all the details you need to get done by quarter, in order for your 1-year, 5-year, and 10-year goals to become a reality. Make sure these goals are in a place where you will see them daily. They must be visible. There is a Harvard study that suggests you are 90% more likely to achieve your goals if you write them down.

Be sure to share your vision board and goals with your team. This will help align your team culture and values around a similar vision and mission. We talked about the importance of establishing your vision and mission, and making it a part of your daily culture. This goes back to hiring the right people. It's impossible to build your dream practice without a strong team of people behind you that desire the same success. Being a healthcare provider and business owner are not one and the same thing. They are 2 very different things. Being a business owner requires you to have smart people around you to help put proper systems in place. You have to come to grips with the fact that you cannot do it all. You have to have other knowledgeable people around you.

Unf*cking Private Healthcare

Which type of knowledgeable people? Well, let's talk about it. You will definitely need a good legal team. Again, which class or classes did you take in college that made you an expert in legal matters? Spend the money on hiring a good lawyer. You need a good accountant (CPA) or a bookkeeper, or both. In Chapter 8, we talked about money management systems and things to help you break through that barrier. Hire a good practice administrator. This is an area you can't afford to be cheap on. When this particular person shares the same vision and mission, they become your biggest advocate in the office for success. As mentioned earlier in this book, make sure they have the skill set, but more importantly, the personality. Spend money on good training for your team. This is a way to advance them as professionals and make them feel part of the process and not just an employee punching the clock. Sales training and customer service will be vital here. And lastly, spend the money on good marketing that helps you get your message out rather than just producing 30 new leads a month. I know what you're thinking: "Trib, that's a shit pot of money to spend."

You're right. It is. Here's what I know, though. There is no shortage of money to be made on this planet. Money is not finite. You can always make more. There is a shortage of really good healthcare practices out there, and if you desire to be one, you need to hire the right people to help you.

There is one other point I have to make when it comes to hiring the right people. Some of you reading this know that you have the wrong people in the wrong position in your practice. You know you do. Part of being a business owner is accepting the responsibility of coaching people up or coaching them the hell out. Nobody likes to be the bad guy and fire someone; however, if your business, and more importantly, other employees, are being affected by a bad egg, it is your duty to make the changes.

A big point I mentioned is spending money on good marketing. What

www.thehealthcareplaybook.com

is good marketing? For me, good marketing is someone who speaks my language; someone who understands what it is like to own a medical business. It is not necessarily someone who has a degree in marketing. Most of the time, people with business degrees, and people with marketing degrees, were taught by other people in colleges, who have never owned a business but like to think that they know how to tell me how to market and run mine. Did you know that the majority of successful business owners on the planet, and successful marketers, don't actually have degrees? Those are the people I want to learn from and work with, and in my opinion, you should too.

Good marketing incorporates your branding and brand messaging into everything you do. It doesn't matter if it's hard marketing or digital marketing. You must, must, must identify the answer to this question first. What's your brand about? Hopefully, during the course of reading this book, you have begun taking steps to answer this question. Without having identified this, you will take on too much input from marketers telling you about your brand rather than you telling them about the message you want to convey. Don't let someone else make up a message for you.

When it comes to marketing and getting referrals, please realize that if you are basing your practice and business growth on referrals from other practices alone, you will have a long uphill battle. You should always have 3 sources of referrals: referrals from other healthcare professionals, referrals from past patients, and direct access referrals. You should have marketing funnels in place to address all these groups. If that statement doesn't make sense to you, go back and read the chapters on marketing again. Whoever is doing your marketing should have systems in place that satisfy all three of these referral areas.

Your social media marketing needs to be on point. I firmly believe that this mode of marketing will be the way in which a majority of people

Unf*cking Private Healthcare

do business in the very near future. Social media is always changing, and so are the demographics on these platforms. Get familiar with them. Learn them, because you will need that knowledge or will need to hire a marketer who has that knowledge, at some point. If you know nothing about it, then anyone can come dazzle you with big terms and fancy dialogue. If you take the time to educate yourself on social media marketing, you will be able to sniff out the bullshit. You don't need to become an expert. You just need to know enough to make sure you hire the right person to do the job for you.

Get involved in the topics of your email campaigns, and understand who they are going to and what the verbiage is to those specific groups of people. Remember the different list of email groups we talked about? You need to know how to talk to each audience. Again, you don't want to have your hands on all of this stuff, because you'll end up working endlessly; but you need to understand why these emails are structured a certain way. I can't tell you how many times I've heard the statement, "Yeah, somebody does this for me, but I have no clue what they actually do."

Palm to face. If you don't know what they're doing or why they're doing it, how do you know if they're doing a good job? Because they said they are? Or because it's converting? What if the conversion could be much higher?

As your marketing develops, and as your team gets better at selling your services and serving your patient base, your revenue will undoubtedly increase. Before it does, you should definitely get a handle on your money savviness. The mishandling of your money will be a huge Achilles heel to your business. You must improve your financial literacy, and set your practice up for financial success. In Chapter 8, I discussed topics like paying yourself, setting up different bank accounts to better manage the flow of money, being aware of the new shiny object you might want to purchase, and above all, cash is king.

www.thehealthcareplaybook.com

Once all these pieces come together, like a puzzle, you will start to see the bigger picture. Hopefully, that picture is the one you have imagined your practice to be like. Maybe it's even better. Again, when you venture from becoming a healthcare provider to being a business owner, you don't know what you don't know. And that's okay. Just don't stay there. Continue to move, and find time to educate yourself beyond the typical continuing education that's required by your medical license. Discover who you are as a business owner, and who you should be as a business owner, and continue to build upon that.

Most healthcare providers who are also business owners, get stuck in this trap of working ungodly hours to make their dream practice happen. You're the doctor and business owner, and you most likely have your hands in every damn thing. I hate to break it to you, but you're not an entrepreneur. At this point, you're self-employed. You hated working for another system, so you opened your own practice because you wanted to do it your way and be your own boss. You no longer do a job to get paid; you own a job to get paid. In order to move from being self-employed to being a business owner, you must put systems into place that no longer make you the owner of a job, but the owner of a system that people work in—a system that you have designed with strong core values, clear vision and mission statements, outstanding customer service, and one that is noticed in your respective market.

All these pieces will make you the owner of your dream practice: a practice that works for you, and not one that consumes your life; a practice that gives you more time and more money in your pocket. Now let's find the motivation to do it, and to keep doing it even when problems arise.

Chapter 10

Finding Motivation – Time to Take Action

After researching motivation and its meaning from several sources, I have come to this collective definition on my own: Motivation is the action or actions we take to experience a desire or avoid a tragedy. Motivation has both an objective and external aspect: a goal or thing you aspire to achieve or have; and an internal or subjective aspect: why you desire to have it or not have it.

Looking at this definition, you should take away 2 very distinct things: objective and subjective reasoning. There is a desire to achieve something, and that something could be tangible or intangible. You could desire a promotion, so you work harder to achieve it. You could be motivated to get over a particular fear, and conquer it. Your goal could be to run a triathlon this year. These are the objects you wish to have. The subjective part of motivation is why you want or desire that particular object. These are typically feelings of satisfaction, achievement, pride, power, security, etc.

In other words, motivation involves emotion. This is important because you must always be aware of your emotions and how they are influencing your actions when you have a goal. Emotions tend be irrational things that cause us to make irrational decisions. Have you ever said something out of anger and immediately regretted it? This is what I mean. As a leader, you must have control of your emotions and have emotional intelligence. I highly recommend you read the book, Emotional Intelligence, by Daniel Goleman. This will help you understand why you feel a certain way, and how to digest that feeling and act in a way that is rational and not emotional. The blame game is an example of this. We all like to point fingers at other external things that are causing us to not reach our goals. We try to change the external instead of looking internally at what we need to change in ourselves. You will not be able to change healthcare as a whole, because that mission requires battling the government and insurance companies, which is quite a large ordeal. Nonetheless, you will point fingers at the system and blame it for your short comings. I have done this too many times. You can, however, change yourself for the betterment of your practice, those who work on your team, and the patients that do business with you.

You have to decide why you are motivated to become a better leader, business owner, and healthcare practitioner. That's what will drive you to do the necessary things to get you to that place you desire, and not get derailed by self-limiting beliefs or what other people may think. I'll use learning to ride a bike as an example. When you are first learning to ride a bike, you are subjected to all kinds of emotions: the physical pain of potentially falling and skinning your knees or elbows; the psychosocial emotion of your friends laughing at you; the satisfaction and joy you expect to feel when you can ride your bike and run around the neighborhood with your friends. Which of these emotions do you think drives success? I'm sure you're resoundingly thinking, the pride and joy of learning to ride, and riding around with your friends. This motivated you as a kid to keep going despite the roadblocks in your way. You took on the challenge despite the failures, and you succeeded. You may have even thought momentarily that you could never do it, but you kept trying and failing, and you succeeded despite those self-limiting thoughts.

Self-limiting beliefs are the stories we often tell ourselves about why we can't achieve certain things. These things hold us back from progressing ourselves. They often originate from what other people tell us about ourselves, such as things like:

www.thehealthcareplaybook.com

"You'll never be able to do that."

"You can't do that."

"That will take too much time and money."

"What makes you think you'll be successful?"

"People will laugh at you."

Chances are, the people who are saying those things are the people who have never done it. Be careful listening to people who give advice on a subject with which they have zero experience. Also be careful of the person who is the avid reader and collector of information but not the implementer. These people have read countless books and journals, and have formulated opinions, but have never taken any action on what they have read or learned. Not everything you learn in life comes from books. Experience often is what paves the way to success. Make the decision to take advice from those who have failed and succeeded, because they have implemented what they have learned. Show me any successful person, and I'll show you a shit ton of failure they experienced before they were successful. Yes, failing is an important part of learning. Failure teaches us what not to do and how to get better the next go around. It took Thomas Edison more than 1,000 attempts to create the light bulb. When asked about it, he said, "Results! I have gotten a lot of results. I know several thousand things that won't work." He didn't fail 1,000 times; he found 1,000 ways it didn't work.

The same is to be said about learning new things in order to become a business owner and a leader. You will have to be okay with being uncomfortable. You will have to be okay with failing. You have to be okay with enjoying the process and taking the little steps it requires to get to where you want to go. The old saying of crawling before walking definitely applies here. You will be faced with challenges and

Unf*cking Private Healthcare

road blocks along the way, and it's how you handle those challenges and road blocks that will keep you motivated to succeed.

Become a problem solver. Many people, when faced with a problem, shut down and don't continue on. Turn your problems into opportunities; opportunities to learn, grow, make mistakes, and keep going. Giving up is where weakness lies. Opportunities and success lie in trying one more time. An example of this, for me, was writing this book. I battled myself constantly in the beginning. I found ways to sabotage myself, with thinking that I couldn't write well enough, and that I wouldn't have the time to do it with everything else that's going on, and wondering if people would really care about what I had to say. I considered hiring a ghost writer that would interview me and my ideas, and put the book together for me. Eventually, through talks with mentors, friends, and family, I overcame these limiting beliefs and was able to put words to paper and write this book in 3 months. I got up early every morning, wrote for 2 hours while everyone else slept, and then went to the office to work at my practice. I spent time on the weekends whenever possible, and sacrificed play time with family and friends to make it happen. Problems forced me to find opportunities to be successful.

Take the necessary educational courses, and read the necessary books available to teach you what you need to know in order to become a better business owner and better leader. I make it my own personal goal to read or listen to, at a minimum, 2 books per month, and to attend at least 2 developmental seminars a year. These are not seminars related to my profession; they are seminars related to personal growth, and growth of my business mentality. A person with low self-awareness and self-worth will spend money on new cars, new homes, fancy vacations, new clothes, new shoes, and other short-term gratifying objects. These people are usually broke. I don't mean broke as in they have no money; I mean broke as in their mindset is such. These people will constantly be in search of the next material thing that only feeds their short-term gratification, leaving them unsatisfied

www.thehealthcareplaybook.com

as a professional, and unsatisfied as a person. A person with high self-awareness and self-worth will spend money on self-education, reading books, going to seminars, learning to do more with less, hiring a business coach, and accepting challenges that make them grow as an individual and a business owner. These people will be rich and wealthy. I don't mean rich in the way of money. Money is nice to have and will yield you more opportunity to live the way you desire. I mean rich as in their lives will be fulfilling. Which one are you? Which do you want to be?

You have to realize that if you do the things that everyone else does, you will get the things that everyone else gets. Are you only getting what is on the surface, or are you getting that which is deeply satisfying? This is where I circle back around to challenging the status quo. Are you okay with where your business is currently? If not, what is your motivation to change it? Is it more time with your family? More money? More knowledge? Personal growth? You must ask yourself who you are now and who it is you need to become to get the things you truly desire for your practice and your life. Then you must ask yourself what it is you need to learn in order to become that person.

I have mentioned several times throughout this book that most healthcare professionals are at least one key skill away from truly being a good business owner. You cannot have your dream practice without making the transition from healthcare professional to business owner. Nor can you make that transition until you are self-aware enough to find the missing pieces, learn those skills, and take the steps to become that person.

I hope this book has given you some actionable items and steps you will take to create your dream business. I have learned a considerable amount in my short time on this Earth, about educating myself on the things I didn't learn in school and college; and the rewards I have received on a personal level are better than any diploma I could ever frame on my wall. The biggest achievement is implementing these

Unf*cking Private Healthcare

concepts into my business and watching it grow, and helping others achieve their goals for their healthcare business; and even more so, offering stellar care to the patients that trust us with their health.

Please be sure to visit www.thehealthcareplaybook.com, and download any of the materials that go along with this book. You can also reach out to me directly via that website, and schedule coaching calls where we can go into depth about your practice and your desires for growth.

I wish each of you success and growth as a professional, business owner, and as a person.

Printed in Great Britain
by Amazon